Fishing for Courage

Mishaps and Magic on Alaska's Outer Coast

Carole Gibb

Quickread Press
Seattle, Washington, USA

Gibb, Carole.
Fishing for Courage: Mishaps and Magic on Alaska's Outer Coast/
Carole Gibb
p. cm.

ISBN 978-0-9858878-0-3

1. Gibb, Carole—Autobiography/Memoir. 2. Alaska, Southeast.
3. Adventure Stories. 4. Travel 5. Island Life and Customs.
6. Fisheries. 7. Women. 8. Creative Thinking. 9. Experiential/
Lifelong Learning.

Summary: An urban woman ends up in a cabin off-the-grid on an Alaska island where she records real-life lessons gained through encounters with bears, storms, and odd sea creatures. Her richest lessons, though, come from her neighbors, mariners who fish for a living, and tell witty stories about their own lives in an outpost that few people, even Alaskans, get to experience.

Cover design by Gery Rudolph
Front cover photo ©Katie Corbin
Back cover photo of author in skiff with Fidget ©Mary Lou Healy
Back cover photo of Fidget ©David Jensen Photography
Back cover photo of author on beach ©Ralph A. Clevenger

To the people of Alaska's Outer Coast.

My heartfelt thanks to all.

A Note to the Reader

For the sake of privacy I altered aspects of this story, and to keep it short I condensed the timeframe. Otherwise, as much as memory and messy notes on bar napkins can be trusted, this is a true story.

To fly we have to have resistance. ~ Maya Lin

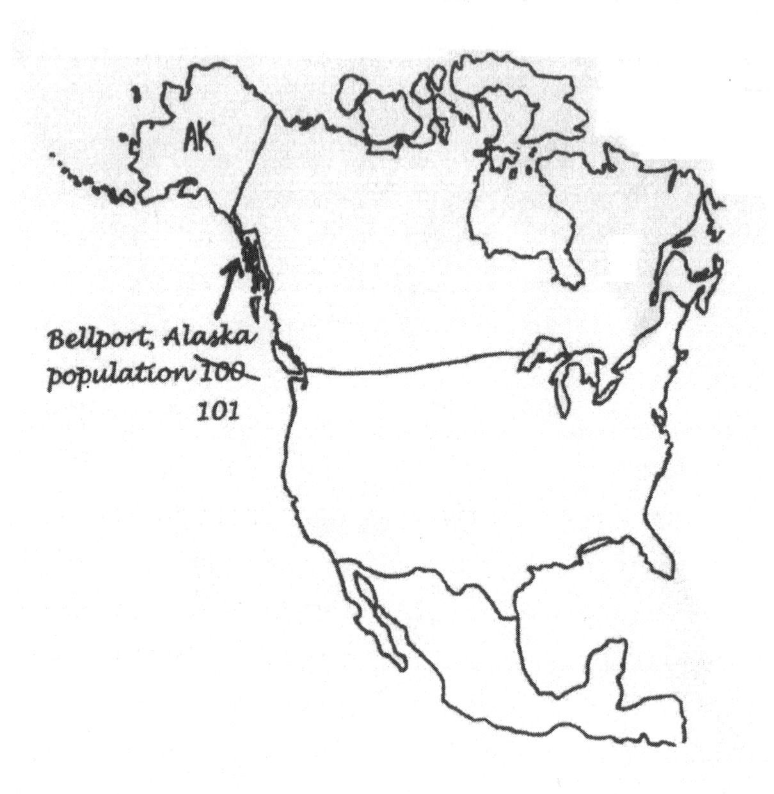
AK
Bellport, Alaska
population 100
101

One

When that first salmon, one hundred feet below, bit the hook and began darting to and fro, it rang a little bell fastened up in the boat's rigging. I engaged the hydraulics and spooled the wire aboard, drawing the fish up toward the surface.

I was on a forty-foot wooden boat, commercial trolling along the jagged, fish-rich coast of Southeast Alaska. While the skipper steered the boat, trying to get our hooks and lures in front of the fish, my job was to bring the fish on board, one at a time, treating each one with care.

A few years shy of forty, I liked my comforts. I was an inexperienced mariner and being around machinery scared me. But people often do things for money that they wouldn't do otherwise.

My plan was to live on this boat July through September, work relentlessly, and walk away at the summer's end with eight, maybe ten thousand dollars. I wanted this wad of cash to help finance a long deferred dream, which was to write a mystery novel.

There it was. A shadowy shape, cutting back and forth just below the water's surface. A silver salmon.

Seeing it gave me an unexpected thrill. I swung the fish on board and stared at it in wonder. Just one fish was all it took. Some primal part of my DNA started to sing.

I thought my attraction to catching fish would be the big surprise of the summer, but it was just the first.

~~~~~

Dear Mary,

Logged eighteen hours on the ocean today, but somehow we managed to catch only forty-one silvers. Each fish earns us under three dollars, so you can imagine the disappointment.

We'd anchored for the night in a natural cove along the rock-strewn edge of the Gulf of Alaska and I was tucked into a corner of the boat with my notebook, writing to Mary, my sister.

Mary was unlike me in every way imaginable—a financial analyst who lived in Atlanta, she was married to a cop and had three kids. But we shared a sweetness of understanding that allowed us to speak our hearts to one another. And better yet, we got each other's jokes.

Fishing will improve, I'm sure. And meanwhile the ocean provides some good entertainment. This morning, I cleaned a salmon and there was a little fish inside, wiggling with indignation—apparently just swallowed. I scooped it overboard and watched it hurry away. I can see the little guy catching up with his buddies and saying, *You're not going to believe what just happened*.
~~~~~

Then we had a humpback whale surface fairly close to the boat. Massive, I thought, when I saw it. Seeing all that latent power gliding along so smooth made my entire body tingle. But then it angled toward us and dove, and the tingles changed to a crawly feeling on the back of my neck, since it looked like it might pass under the boat.

We turned to give it some room, but even so it resurfaced uncomfortably close. It came up and blew, *whoooosh*—and the misty breath floated right onto me.

Cool, you might think. Well, think again, because it smelled putrid. Somebody should tell that whale to brush its baleen!

Until this stinky whale breath incident I never appreciated how, even though we're dealing with fish blood and guts all the time, the boat just smells like ocean and air. Never even a whiff of that rank fishy smell. That smell apparently occurs when fish oil oxidizes, which is why I'm constantly hosing down the deck and, at the end of the day, scrubbing with bleach.

Speaking of guts I'd like to state for the record that the goo inside a fish is squishy, but less messy than one might expect. It's arranged in this sensible package—you make three quick slices with a well-placed blade, grip and pull, and the works come out in a sort of balloon. Overboard it goes, all in one motion. Well, ideally anyway. I have flung guts pretty much all over the boat because I get excited and lose focus.

Today, we quit around ten p.m. and charged to one of the little semi-protected indents that dot the Gulf of Alaska coast. Charging means going top speed, but a troller's top speed is only about eight knots (a hair over eight mph), so it's not like restraint harnesses are required.

We negotiated around a bunch of rocks to enter this little cranny in the coast called Peril Cove. Tom dropped the anchor and cut the engine. When it humped out its last cough it was as though my ears had been hot and thirsty all day, and the silence settled on them like a deep, cold drink.

Glad to be off duty, I played with the dog, Fidget, tossing a carrot around the deck for her to fetch. She's a graceful dog, with a silky black body and a tan face, chest, and legs. Tom recently rescued her from the pound and though I've never been around dogs much, or even cared to be, she's pretty sweet.

Ocean-caught fish for dinner. You'd think eating so much fish would get boring, but it's gorgeous food and my body seems to know it. I'll go further and confess that eating wild fish makes me feel sort of wild myself, inside. Fidget chases her tail out of sheer giddy happiness, and sometimes Mary, I swear I feel like doing the same.

Okay, my eyelids are drooping. I'll write more later!

xxoo

Carole

PS: You asked how it's going with Tom. Things are good. We're working out well on the boat.

In her last letter she'd inquired about me and Tom. It was an apt question since couples often have trouble working together. But he and I had been sweethearts for years and ours was a comfortable, elastic relationship. He was a stocky, smiling, huggable guy, although when fishing started he turned more serious, less huggy. Past summers I'd remained in Juneau while he went fishing, and I hardly heard from him. It was a normal part of the commercial fishing life and I didn't take it personally. When the season was open, romance falls off the radar. So whether I was in Juneau or beside Tom on the boat, I knew the drill: it was work now, play later.

~~~~~

Deckhands, especially new ones, can get nauseous in the fish hold and my first time down in the belly of the boat, I understood why. My body was getting jerked back and forth as though I'd fallen inside a washing machine. The waves against the boat's hull made a sloshing sound that echoed in the cave-like space, worsening the sensation.

The wild salmon we caught were destined for fine restaurants and upscale fish markets, which meant that after landing and cleaning fish we had to get their temperature down quickly, but it had to be done without marring their surprisingly tender scales. So I faced the task of gently layering our catch on ice, one by one, and sprinkling ice around each one.

I sat there, fighting nausea, telling myself I was on an amusement park ride, but was getting paid for the thrill. My bottom kept sliding a bit to the left, then to the right, but after a few minutes, I'd melted a tiny hollow in the ice and stopped moving so much.

I took a salmon into my gloved hands. Maybe it was the backdrop of the glittering white ice, but I noticed something I hadn't seen before. The scales of these fish were truly beautiful. Though primarily silver, they also glinted with jewel-like flashes of purple, aqua, and green.
~~~~~

Wild salmon hatch in a fresh-water stream, live three or four years out on the ocean, and return to their origin stream where they spawn once and die. The dry scientific facts are simple.

But written on those colorful scales, I saw the story of a life, a story that began before this fish even existed. Four years ago, in the spring, the snow melted and rushed off the mountains. It swelled the streams and put out a scent, calling mature salmon in from the wide ocean. After a harrowing trip upstream, past eagles and bears, otters and fishermen, a pair of salmon spawned. Minuscule eggs buried in the stream gravel started to grow. And this particular fish, the one now in my hands, emerged months later from the gravel as a fry. It grew up to live a free and fishy life, roaming all over the sea.

And when the time was right, some drive inside the fish, combined with that hint of spring snowmelt in the ocean, drew it back to the fresh water stream of its birth.

It comforted me that we caught these salmon at the end of their life cycle, right before they were going to die anyway. And I liked that fisheries biologists and a state advisory board ensured that a healthy percentage of fish got through to spawn, and kept the cycle going, before we were allowed to take our share.

Sitting in the fish hold, growing numb from the cold, a little hope bloomed in my heart that whoever ate this fish would do so with a special kind of pleasure. Even if they gave no conscious thought to its life story, maybe some part inside of them would thrill to the wildness that formed it.

~~~~~

Those first few weeks I was deeply happy to be fishing. The work touched a chord inside me. But there were a couple of clouds smudging the horizon.

The price per pound we got for our silvers was well under a dollar; the lowest Tom had ever seen it. Apparently, it had to do with farmed fish flooding the market. The price was expected to go up—it always did as the summer progressed—so we could count on better wages ahead. But those first weeks our earnings were painfully meager.

Compounding this was another issue. We couldn't seem to catch many fish.

The state fish and game bureau does a thorough job of managing commercial fisheries, so we knew the cause wasn't depleted stocks. Tom said he wanted to determine if other boats were doing poorly, or if it was just us. If other fishermen were also experiencing low catch rates we'd know the fish were just running late, or had shifted slightly north or south to travel in currents that were more feed-rich.

Finding out how other boats were performing, though, wasn't as simple as just asking.

Dear Mary,

We're on our way to anchor up. There wasn't much scrubbing to do since we hardly caught anything. It poured all day, plus there was a steady wind with a bite to it. In July.

I ducked inside the pilothouse to thaw out every few hours. Tom's not much into conversation lately, so
~~~~~

mostly we listened to the "VHF." This is what he calls the marine radio, and I'm trying to remember to call it that, too, but I accidentally keep saying "VHS" instead.

"VHF, very high frequency," he patiently says.

"Oh, right," I nod as if that means something to me, while secretly thinking, *very happy fruit fly*, and *virile hunky flirt*, trying to lodge those letters V-H-*F* into my brain.

So the reason we're listening to the radio is to pick up hints on whether nearby boats are catching. The thing is, fishermen don't like to disclose their catch rates, or how deep they fish, or what type of lures they favor, or what they had for breakfast, or when they last changed their socks, or how they feel about cauliflower. In other words, they're secretive, these fishermen.

Certain skippers, the successful ones, have coding partners—other successful people with whom they share catch data via the VHF. But since everyone monitors the radio, hungry to learn where the bite is, partners must be wily. Their secret codes can sound funny. One guy will say, "I have a few more than a . . ." There will be a rustle of paper while he refers to his key sheet of codes, and he'll finally say, "smoky brown cow." Then his partner will say, "I've got a candied ham," and the first guy replies, "Sounds good with eggs."

Other fishermen hide their codes in casual conversation. Rather than saying, "I have a such-n-such fill-in-the-code-name," they sneak code words in on the sly. Tom told me about a couple of guys who talked gardening all last season and nobody knew whether they were using it for a cover, or really liked gardening, or both.

We're not coding with anyone, but some friends invited us to a barbecue tonight on their boat, so after we "set the hook" (that means anchor, matey!) we'll row over in the dinghy. We'll get dinner, but we're also going to get the scuttlebutt. I'll let you know what we learn.

xxoo

Carole

Unfortunately, the scuttlebutt indicated that we *were* doing poorly compared to other boats. I fretted to Tom that it was me, jinxing us. Maybe the salmon could sense my desire. Maybe my lust for catching fish was traveling down the wire and radiating off our hooks, and that made the fish veer away, as though warned off by a bad scent.

Tom said I wasn't jinxing us.

Then I wondered if my lack of experience was causing the trouble. I tripped and hit my head a lot. Maybe my head-thunking scared the fish off. Tom reassured me head-thunking happened on boats all the time, and fish didn't seem especially sensitive to that.

The weeks stacked up and we tried not to buckle under these two stresses—few fish and a distressingly low price. We worked harder, we changed areas, we stayed in the same spot, we asked advice, we kept to ourselves—we tried it all—but nothing seemed to help. Despite the long days and unflagging effort, we were barely making enough to cover fuel.

Dear Mary,

I can handle the wet, the cold, and how few fish we're catching. The worst thing, and it is nearly unbearable, is how hard it is to make a fashion statement out here.

Every day, I waddle around in the same outfit: rubber rain bibs, oversized rubber raincoat, and XtraTufs—the rubber boots everybody wears. They come to the knee, have a good tread on slippery decks, and are excessively clumpy. I think BF Goodrich makes them.

Footwear made by a tire company. Now do you see why I feel somewhat less than chic?

I tore the page out of my notebook and crumpled it in a tight ball. The happy mood of the initial weeks on the boat was gone. I had managed to write a letter pretending otherwise, but couldn't send it because it was a lie. Letter-writing always required one thing from me: that I dig down and try to speak the truth.

Hey Mary,

The money sucks . . . but at least the hours are long.

xxoo
Carole

This single sentence, this tiny touch of honesty, made it impossible to pretend there was much hope for my goal for the summer, which was to get ahead financially.

The real problem, though, ran deeper than money. My interest in the fishing life had become stronger than I even knew. Wanting something that makes emotional sense but goes against logic spells trouble. But it can also raise some interesting questions. What constitutes wealth, aside from money? What's true security? If you always have to whisper *righty-tighty-lefty-loosey* when using a screwdriver, does that mean you're dense?

Questions like these loomed ahead of me, but when I wrote this single line, this wry lament to my sister, I had no idea. I was just trying to get at the truth. But the truth has a peculiar power, a sort of momentum to it. One truth leads to another, and that takes you to the next. It's the kind of thing that can be disruptive to plans, especially if the plans have to do with arranging a calm, tidy life.

Two

Tom stuck his head out of the pilothouse door and told me, "Stack 'em." This was his signal for me to bring the gear on deck. The fishing day was over.

He throttled up and aimed our bow toward Skookum Bay. It wasn't the closest place to anchor but was behind a point of land that offered shelter from the fitful winds predicted that night.

Dinner was a wordless, sad affair, and when that meal—always my favorite—failed to lift my spirits, I knew it was time to talk.

After dinner, Tom went to sit up on the fly bridge, atop the pilothouse. I climbed up the ladder to join him and we sat there, slapping at no-see-ums, wondering what to say.

I looked around, taking in the view. We had a sky streaked with orange and purple, and a pair of eagles that circled into view, riding a thermal. Deep green forest surrounded the bay's expansive, calm, black-green water.

"I guess we need to talk," I finally said.

"Okay," he said.

Up to this point I'd done no deep thinking, I'd just come to realize something had to change. With so few fish coming on board Tom didn't need a deckhand, nor did he need to kiss fifteen percent of his earnings good-bye. As for me, my cherished goal of becoming an author required a certain amount of start-up money, and that was not happening. So here we were.

Drawing in a deep breath, I let the words come. "I love fishing more than I expected . . ." I paused and sought his eyes, but he was looking down. "But maybe I should consider getting off the boat. Does that make sense, or . . . ?" My throat got tight so I stopped.

He met my eyes for the first time in what seemed like years and a hint of something, relief maybe, showed on his face. "It's probably for the best," he said.

Something in me collapsed, and jolts of disappointment and anger shot through me. Not anger at Tom, I told myself, but at circumstances. Well okay, partly at Tom. Why did he have to be so quick to agree? Why couldn't he say what I wanted to hear, something along the lines of, *"Oh no, don't leave the boat, Carole, you're doing everything absolutely right. The reason we're not catching? Oh that—it's merely an electrical current thing; we're repelling fish rather than attracting them. All I have to do is reverse the current and we're going to be loading up our lines for the rest of the season. Well, I'm really glad we talked . . ."*

"I'm sorry," Tom said, and any anger I had toward him dissolved.

"Me, too," I said and climbed below to my bunk. I lay

there prickling with anxiety. I tried to picture what would happen, going forward, and felt myself floundering. Returning to Juneau made the most sense in terms of finding work, since I had plenty of contacts there. But I'd rented my house out for the summer. Ousting my renters was out of the question, so I'd have to find a place to live. Juneau was in the middle of a housing shortage, so rent would be high.

The appeal of fishing, aside from what a person earned, was that you spent nothing. You lived on the boat, your food was paid for, and all you did was fish, so you saved money normally spent on entertainment, car gas, impulse buys, all that. It was a great way to get ahead.

But now, that pile of money I hoped to earn this summer wasn't going to manifest, and on top of that, once I set foot in Juneau my bank account was going to start hemorrhaging. Before I even got there, in fact, because chartering a seat to Juneau on a floatplane was going to cost more than a hundred bucks.

I hugged a pillow tight against my chest and groaned with frustration. From the time I was old enough to hold a pencil to a notebook I expected to grow up to be an author. But during my twenties and half of my thirties other pursuits captivate me—travel, men, partying, adventure—they all beckoned. I wrote articles for newspapers and magazines, but never any fiction.

But a few years ago the obvious started to sink in: we only get so much time on this earth, and I was burning through mine without doing the one thing I wanted to do.

Most people I knew who were closing in on forty had built substantial careers, or were half paid off on their mortgages, or were raising families, whereas I'd spent my time traveling from place to place, like a skipping stone, never sinking in, never investing in anything. The urge to write books rose up in me like a one-hundred-year flood, changing my entire geography.

I ran into a snag, however. A lot of people can work a job for money and write a novel at the same time, but it became evident that I'm not one of them. I tried, but could not split my attention like that. So I came up with a complicated, but doable, plan. I had a house in Juneau that was in spectacularly bad shape. Rather than just fix it, I decided to carve its three floors into apartments. Once that was done, I'd inhabit the smallest corner of the house and live off the rental income while trying to write my mystery novel.

For two years I put every ounce of spare time and effort into the house project, but things inched along at a glacial pace. I wanted to pull off this massive remodel without going into correspondingly massive debt, which put a drag on things.

So I came up with this current twist—the deckhanding scheme. My plan was to fish for a couple of summers and work on the remodel during the winters. That concentration of summer cash and winter effort promised to accelerate things nicely. I'd be just turning forty, and set for life.

And at the start of the summer, my plan appeared to dovetail so beautifully with reality. I caught that first fish and knew: I was going to love making my money this way.

Except, now this fishing thing had flopped.

Another groan rumbled out of me. I stuffed my pillow under my head, promised myself I'd feel better in the morning, and made my escape into slumber.

~~~~~

In the morning I felt worse. I stared into space, letting my coffee cup turn cold in my palm while Tom pulled the anchor. He aimed us toward the nearest port, Belltown, so I could charter a floatplane to take me back to civilization.

A few hours later we were skirting the edge of large, mountainous island. This island, the size of Delaware, was home to less than two thousand people. Most of them lived on the island's far side which was less exposed to the volatile Gulf of Alaska.

On the side that was battered by the gulf, a twenty-mile inlet sliced like an incision into the island. Bellport, a fishing enclave of about one hundred souls, clung to the shore of this inlet.

All morning I'd remained slumped in my chair, inert. Noticing this, Tom suggested that I take a little recovery time at his cabin before going back to Juneau. He was referring to the cabin he used as his shore camp. It had a pantry full of food, he said, along with bookshelves full of reading. And if fishing turned around and suddenly got busy, I'd be in position to jump back on the boat. You never know, he said, but we might end up having a great season, after all.
~~~~~

Watching the green shore slide by, I thought about Tom's idea. My need for a rest seemed obvious now that he pointed it out. The other thing he said—that the fishing could get better and still provide us both with an income—this caught me by surprise. He hadn't expressed any of this optimism while on the flybridge the night before. But then, once I thought about it, I understood.

Working on the ocean, a person's heart seesawed between hope and despair. It happened many times a day. One minute the bell is ringing like crazy; you've caught twenty beautiful glinting fish and you're ecstatic. But then you discover that sea lions are following the boat and have begun plucking salmon off your hooks as fast as they climb on. You have no choice but to pull your gear and leave, right when you're in the fish.

An hour later, smiling porpoises cheer you up with their games, slicing across your bow, jumping into the air with joy, but then *bam*, suddenly a wad of kelp twists your lines up in a knot. You're forced to cut loose your gear and watch it sink. Now you're losing money instead of making it.

And these are just the little things. There are also the big ones. You can have a couple of weeks in which you luck into unbelievable numbers of fish. Debts that have hung over you for years look like they'll be paid off. But in just minutes, things can turn. A rogue wave can appear out of nowhere. It can break out your pilothouse window, drench your electronics, sweep you overboard. Or you notice the boat is listing to port, you go below, discover a plank has sprung loose of its fastenings, and oh dear God, now you're sinking.

So it's no wonder a person's mood swings all over. Convictions out on the ocean become as unpredictable as the waves, the weather, and the wild fish themselves.

Thinking about all this, I felt my hopes stir. Hope wasn't a particularly logical thing to feel in the face of all this uncertainty, but there it was.

I started to wonder if just getting off the boat could be enough for now. With two people on board, the lack of fish was twice as depressing, the income-to-work ratio doubly dismal. But like Tom said, the fishing could pick up. Then it would make sense—money sense—to have two people slinging those silvers on board.

But Tom's cabin wasn't actually in Bellport. It was down the inlet on a lonely cove accessible only by boat. The cove wasn't tied to Bellport's power or water systems, so everything at the cabin, from electricity to plumbing to heat, had to be configured and maintained by hand. And the way Tom configured and maintained everything wasn't especially logical, unless you knew the fifteen considerations you couldn't possibly know without his history with the place.

I'd spent time with him at the cabin over the years and it had always felt like an adventure, but a key difference was that it had been a guided adventure. To stay there without him as my capable host would be altogether different.

On the brink of canning the idea and telling him no way, I remembered something that fishermen liked to say. They repeated it like a mantra: You get your good stretches and your bad, but pushing through the bad times—persistence—that's what earned you the mother lode. That's how you got to sweet city.

I wanted to get to sweet city. If I returned to Juneau without staying around a bit longer, it would always bug me, not knowing what could have happened if I'd persisted.

Plenty of humans, right this very second, were stepping outside their comfort zones, I reminded myself. Starting a relationship, starting a family, going back to school, retiring, moving, quitting drugs, taking a big trip, launching a business.

And in situations where people face new territory, careful calculations and leaps of faith, combined, probably led to more success than either one or the other alone.

So, by the time we pulled into Bellport, I'd decided to take a leap of faith and stick around, for a while at least.

THREE

WE SLID THE FISHING BOAT into a stall in the Bellport harbor, climbed into Tom's seventeen-foot open skiff and motored promptly out of town. The plan was to settle me in—his cabin was not far down the coast—then he would steam right back out to the fishing grounds. Though we would have liked more time together on shore, the season spanned only so many days, and until it ended, fishing took priority.

He sat in the stern, gripping the outboard tiller to steer, and told me that if the fishing picked up he'd call me on the VHF and say "backhoe"—slip it into the conversation casually so no one knew he was catching lots of fish. And this secret code word would be my signal to jump in the skiff and rendezvous with him out at the fish buyer's barge.

"Okay," I said. I was huddled on the skiff's middle seat, trying not to flinch as the wind threw needles of rain at me. The dog, Fidget, crouched between us looking as robust and cheery as I felt: Her wet fur was plastered down and her ears and tail were clamped tight against her body.

Ravens, eagles, and jumping fish were the only other

creatures we saw. We rounded a point and there was Steep Cove, a mile-long crescent in the shore dotted with a handful of cabins.

We landed on the beach in front of the cabin, unloaded, and tied the skiff onto an outhaul. The outhaul was a line on pulleys that ran out to an anchor set in the water and back to shore again. We secured the skiff to the line, and "hauled it out." So this way, when the tide withdrew two times a day, our mode of transport stayed afloat and available for use. Keeping the skiff afloat, safe from the ever-changing tide was akin to keeping gas in the car. You had to be mindful of it or else you'd be immobilized.

We went inside the sixteen-by-twenty-four-foot cabin. The air was about fifty degrees and damp. One good thing about the cabin was despite the damp, the cracks in the floor let air circulate, so it never smelled moldy. The front half of the cabin faced onto the inlet. It was just one room, with a vaulted white ceiling and a wall that was mostly windows, making it the largest-feeling small room I'd ever been in. The back half, pressed against a cliff, held the kitchen and a bathroom with a tub and toilet. Above the kitchen was the sleeping loft. In the middle where the front room met with the back, a big-bellied woodstove squatted beside a tall water tank wrapped in silver insulation blanket.

Tom's first task was to "start the water," which involved lugging a five-gallon bucket bristling with tools up the treacherous creek beside the cabin and doing something to a waterline that concerned valves and siphons and such.

I knelt before the woodstove, took a deep breath, and

tried to start a fire. Now, some people gain fire-making skills when young, on family campouts or the like, while others seem to be born with a gene in their DNA that tells them what to do. I had missed out on both counts, so on previous visits to the cabin I'd happily left it to Tom, never dreaming I'd be staying here without him.

He came back into the cabin a half hour later to get another tool. I threw him an exasperated look and said the obvious: "I couldn't get a fire going."

Scratching his elbow absently, he said, "That's good, actually. We can't start a fire until I get the water running or we'll melt the hot water coils inside the stove."

It took me a minute to grasp his meaning and then I had to laugh. I'd almost melted a part of the cabin's water system but my inability to make a fire saved us!

Tom, whistling, got the water gushing into the sink and then knelt before the woodstove to light a fire. I watched. When done, he gave me a look that said: *See? It's easy.* Pride made me nod sagely, as if the veil of ignorance had been lifted. But it was about as clear to me as a magician's trick.

Next, he changed out the propane bottle, which was almost out, so I wouldn't have to deal with it myself. Propane ran the kitchen range and a light mounted above the armchair. Also, for those rare times it was too warm to start the woodstove, a propane-fueled water heater stood ready.

Tom gave me some pointers on the cabin's twelve-volt electrical system—it powered the cabin's VHF radio and some lights—and then he showed me how to fuel up and start the generator to charge the batteries.

He began to gather supplies to take back to the boat—more peanut butter, some oil filters, a fresh supply of books—and I curled up in the cabin's single armchair over by the window, trying to suppress my shivers. I was chilled and worn-out from emotion, but the real problem was this: I felt intimidated by the cabin's crazy water system and the stubborn woodstove. And the propane lights that woofed up in a big flame when you lit them. I couldn't even call Tom's cell phone on the boat if I had questions because the cabin *had no phone.* This was a detail I'd forgotten but it suddenly loomed huge.

Some small object digging into my rear distracted me from my angst over the cabin's nonexistent phone. I shifted my weight to the side and reached in the chair cushion to unearth the thing. It was a bullet for Tom's rifle. The cabin was on the messy side, with random things everywhere, so finding a rifle round in the chair's folds was no big surprise.

Absentmindedly, I ran my fingers over the brass casing and stared outside. The inlet, a fiord that cut a mile wide and twenty miles long, spread out in front of the cabin, black and deep. Across the inlet, mountains shot out of the water and rose at a ludicrously steep angle before capping out at thirty-five-hundred feet. They weren't the tallest mountains I'd seen, but because they loomed so close and appeared so nearly vertical, they were the most commanding.

I got up and stood before the window. If I craned my neck and looked sideways another Steep Cove cabin was visible down the beach, but I couldn't walk there—the land was too steep. Looking the other way, I couldn't see any signs of humanity, because cliffs obscured the view. Bellport was less than a mile in that direction, but reaching it on foot wasn't an option. Once, a group of Tom's friends got it into their heads to climb over from Bellport to visit him on foot. It took them hours and one woman broke her arm along the way.

The bullet slipped from my fingers and dropped.

"Uh . . ." Tom said. I glanced over and he gestured at the bullet on the floor between my feet. "It's probably not a good idea to drop it like that."

"What?"

"On its primer. A piece of gravel on the floor, and it could . . . well . . . *bam!*"

I really hate explosions, or even the slightest suggestion of one. Shrilly I told Tom, "You can't leave me here by myself!"

He came over and hugged me, offering assurances that I'd be fine.

"But I don't know anything about . . ." I waved my arms in a big arc, "anything." The setting was so foreign I didn't even know what, specifically, to worry about. I rambled on about how I was afraid of blowing myself up while he remained cheerfully upbeat about my ability to avoid doing that.

When our neighbor's skiff pulled up—Tom was hitching a ride back to the harbor—I wanted to fling myself down, clutch onto his ankles, and beg him not to leave.

Sensing my trepidation he said soothingly, "If you have any questions call me on the VHF."

The cabin's radio didn't reach most of the places he fished, I reminded him.

"If you can't reach me," he said, "John and Betty always have their radio on. You can call them." John and Betty were a couple in their seventies who lived in Bellport, and Tom considered them dear friends. "They'll help in a heartbeat," he said, and then he was gone.

~~~~~

The silence in the cabin roared in my ears. I sat by the window and willed myself to think of the bright side. At least I had a big king salmon fillet lying on ice in a cooler, and Tom had left the dog, so I wasn't completely alone.

Fidget sat by my knees. Her ears were half-perked and she stared intently at my face with the biggest, most trusting brown eyes. Actually, they looked sort of worried. But she kept them pinned to me as if she believed I knew the answers to her questions. *Oh you sweet dog*, I thought, *you might want to find someone else to look at with those eyes.*

Tom had urged me to radio John and Betty if I had questions, but the VHF was monitored by *everyone*—nearby boats as well as people onshore—and mostly for entertainment.

I could just hear myself: "John? Betty? Come in, please. Have you seen a skiff float by? I don't see ours on the outhaul anymore. Darn it all, my shoelace knot must have come undone."

I gave Fidget a pat on her warm head and crawled into the loft to sleep. The loft had about four feet of clearance at its highest point and sloped sharply down from there.
~~~~~

A window, propped wide open, saved it from being claustrophobic.

It was early evening, only about eight, and through the window streamed the hearty Alaska summer light, the kind that wouldn't fade until around midnight, but I felt whipped and just wanted the day to end. I could hear Fidget pacing at the foot of the ladder and said some reassuring words to her. Suddenly I heard dog toenails scrabbling up the ladder and she popped up through the hole into the loft.

I put an old blanket under the eave, right alongside the mattress, and she curled up there. My hand crept out to rest on her shoulder. In the midst of so much wilderness just having another heart beating next to mine helped calm me. She gave a little sigh, as though she felt it too, and soon we were both sound asleep.

~~~~~

I opened my eyes to a darkness that felt like a blinding weight against my eyes. I could hear Fidget next to me, puffing out soft doggie breaths, and could also hear, through the open window, the tiniest sound of water lapping against the shore.

I angled myself so I could look outside. The buoy marking the rocks off Fork Island, a distant pinprick of light, flashed once every second. Other than that, blackness prevailed. Any direction I turned my eyes, save a few points on the compass, was complete wilderness. The person I was in my twenties, the young me, would have found this thrilling. But I wanted this to be the productive time in my
~~~~~

life, and to lie in this loft listening to my heart hammer was not productive. It made me think of a ticking clock, which made me think about everything I was not doing. I was not making money, I was not getting any work done on my house, and I wasn't getting one bit closer to putting that novel down on paper. I had goals to pursue, so no, I wasn't thrilled to be here, stalled out on the side of the road. Way off the road, actually.

Suddenly I sat up, cracking my head on the sloped loft ceiling. *Idiot! Use this time to work on your mystery.* I switched on the twelve-volt light beside the bed and tried jotting some plot ideas in my notebook. There was nothing to distract me—no Internet to surf, no movie to watch, no phone—and I couldn't concentrate.

I thought about those women authors you heard about who got out of bed and wrote diligently from four a.m. to six a.m. at the kitchen table, before their twenty babies woke up and started wailing for breakfast. Instead of helping, this just made me feel like more of a loser.

Tossing my notebook aside, I picked up a magazine and a quote by Rachel Carson caught my eye: "Those who dwell among the beauties and mysteries of the earth are never alone or weary of life."

Rach, I thought, *you got a lot of things right, but not this.* I'd never felt so alone, and the beauties of the earth weren't helping. On the boat I'd taken Tom's constant company for granted, and had even grown a little tired of it. But having the opposite now—no company at all—felt like an ache. It felt like not being allowed to sleep, or eat, or breathe oxygen.

I grabbed for my notebook.

Dear Mary,

I'm taking a break at the Steep Cove cabin since there isn't enough work for me on the boat. It's a bit lonely at the moment. I wish you were here.

I know what to do. I'm going to imagine you're coming for a visit. I'll describe what you would experience on your way here, and thus conjure myself up some company. The most affordable trip to Alaska, ever!

So, first, you'd check in at the Juneau airport small-planes desk. You would get in a shuttle van, go to a pond and climb into a floatplane. You'd be sitting amidst bags of U.S. mail, and your pilot would be a charming red-haired man with a fake leg.

The plane, about the size of a VW bus, would taxi to the end of the pond and take off. It would drone along at about five hundred, maybe a thousand feet, carrying its bulbous floats like a bumblebee loaded with pollen.

This region of Alaska is called the Panhandle. It's a five-hundred-mile strip of islands dangling off Alaska's lower right corner. Your floatplane would fly over a bunch of islands and saltwater fjords, bays, and channels. You'd look for signs of humankind but see few. You might, however, see a whale throw its massive self up out of the water, twist sideways, and then crash back down with a big splash.

People debate why whales breach. I'm convinced they do it for fun. Self-expression, man. To feel their senses tingle. I'd be breaching all the time if I were a whale, since tingling senses are a favorite thing of mine.

After about forty-five minutes you'd catch sight of open ocean, the Gulf of Alaska, glimmering across the entire horizon. Locals refer to this long, wild border between ocean and shore as the Outer Coast, and the words are spoken with a certain reverence.

The Outer Coast has a peculiar allure. It calls on people to make their living from the water. It calls them for work and also for play, and compels them to seek the places their parents and grandparents have gone before, questing after fish and berries and deer.

But sis, here I'll diverge from my glossy brochure tone to give you the mean truth: It's beautiful, but has vicious weather and rock-studded waters. And practically every year somebody dies, or comes close to it. Sorry, but I just needed to throw in that bit of reality.

Now back to the glossy brochure tone: your pilot would reach an island and would turn and fly between mountains pressing close on either side to follow a saltwater inlet. And there it would be: Bellport. From the air it resembles a stubborn barnacle, a bumpy white dot clinging to the edge of the inlet.

The floatplane would land in the boat harbor. You'd climb out, jump in the skiff with me, and we'd skim down the coast to this cabin. I'd cook you a dinner of fresh king salmon, mashed potatoes, and canned sweet corn. This meal sounds simple but you would swoon.

I stopped writing to shake the cramp out of my hand and noticed the letter had done its magic; my heart felt at ease.

I'm sleepy now and not nearly so lonesome, sis. I'll say good night and thanks. Give your boys a smooch for me.

xxoo
Carole

FOUR

THE FOLLOWING DAY it poured rain so I stayed in the cabin. I cracked open my notebook a half-dozen times, trying to turn myself into a novelist, but couldn't bend my mind to it. I ended up loafing around, reading.

Every so often I got hit with the longing for chocolate. The cabin shelves were stocked with canned goods and dry goods, but no chocolate. Buying some in town was an option but I didn't feel up to it. Some days I can tackle unfamiliar things, like starting the skiff, boating into town, and parking there in the harbor with people watching. I called them can-do days. But this wasn't one of them.

The tide licked in, gently swirling against the cabin pilings beneath the front windows, and then eased back out again.

I looked up from my reading and saw, perhaps thirty feet from the window, a whiskered sea otter. He floated on his back with small pile of clams and mussels on his stomach. He gripped a rock in his paw and clacked the rock against the shells to break them open, then scooped the delectables into his mouth. He paused to drift for a bit, chewing—I could see his whiskers waggling—then flipped and dove out of sight.

Slick, I thought, *no dirty dishes!*

Later, when it was time to crawl up in the loft, sleep came mercifully quick. But I woke in the night to a windstorm flinging rain in at me through the open window. Yanking the window closed, I wiped the water off my face, and listened to a cacophony of strange noises—trees whooshing, squeaks and clangs from things on the porch, and snapping sounds, a tarp probably.

Determined to get back to sleep, I got the old imagination fired up and pictured Mary sleeping in the front room on the cabin's substitute for a couch, a wonderfully tacky beanbag chair encased in fake zebra fur. The image made me smile, and despite the storm's tumult, I fell back asleep.

By morning the weather had turned misty and peaceful, and I woke up knowing it was a can-do day. I drank some high-test coffee, ate a bowl of Cheerios and pulled on my rubber outfit, ready to make the trip into Bellport. Two desires filled me. I yearned to see other humans and I had to find some chocolate.

Fidget stayed close on my heels—she wasn't about to let me go out the door without her. But outside we encountered a surprise.

The night's windstorm had dropped a big hemlock onto the beach. Its mess of branches—and a gnarly mess it was—had landed on the skiff's outhaul.

We weren't going anywhere; at least, not until I freed the outhaul line.

A handsaw would have freed the outhaul line from the clutches of the fallen tree, but it would have taken me at least a week. With Tom's guidance I'd once made a few cuts with a chainsaw and that was the extent of my chainsaw experience.

I forced myself to go find the chainsaw. I explained to Fidget that this was what people called a learning experience, and taking a deep breath, I went to work.

Dear Mary,

A person rarely thinks of their femoral vein, let alone appreciates it, but today I'm filled with relief that mine's still intact.

I had to use the chainsaw—it's too complicated to explain why—and at first it didn't go too badly. There was that part about starting it, which was awkward, and then, flustered, I couldn't remember whether the chain should be spinning when it touched the tree branch (yes) or if you should wait and pull the trigger after you touch it to the thing you want to cut (very definitely no).

But I got the hang of it, and things went fairly well.

Except I had no idea how wobbly my arms were getting. I cut and cut and cut, and there was just one last branch to get. It was at shoulder level, so I heaved the chainsaw up to finish the job. The saw chewed through and the branch dropped down, as expected. But the saw dropped down as well, because my arms gave out. The bar swung down and grazed my leg before I could yank it back up.

It only cut through my jeans and etched a slight scratch. I'm looking at the scratch right now—the very place the teeth would have chewed into my thigh had I been a millisecond slower.

I could have ended up being an example of natural selection at work. What an embarrassing way to go.

I'll sign off for now. More later.

xxoo

Carole

I closed the notebook, still upset by the incident and not sure how to feel better, but then my mind whispered the word *chocolate*. The positive glow this caused inside me made me realize if I ever wanted to write a survival manual it could probably be just two words: administer chocolate.

Grabbing some money, I whistled for Fidget and skiffed into town for a fix. I got to the harbor where the wind was calm and the water's surface shone like a glassy mirror, and still I managed to crash-land the skiff. And of the hundred or so people living in Bellport, about half of them happened to be standing around to see me do it.

I lunged for the tie-up cleat, fumbled around with my lines, and finally got things secured. I tried to keep my composure, which wasn't easy because I felt like shouting: Listen everyone, I'm not always this inept! I can be in my *car*, on a hill, in a snowstorm, checking for food on my face in the rearview mirror and *whip* into a parallel parking spot, okay?

I pressed my lips together, gave the line an extra wrap around the cleat, and stomped up the harbor ramp.

The ramp led directly to Bellport's main "street" which wasn't a street at all, but a twelve-foot-wide boardwalk built atop tall pilings. This boardwalk formed the very heart of town and was a prime example of how intrepid humans can be when they decide to carve their existence out on an island that lacked, among other things, level land.

Wood-frame buildings lined the boardwalk on both sides. On the water's side they perched on pilings, safely above seawater that rose as much as twelve feet on tides twice a day. On the other side of the boardwalk, structures pressed their backs against the steep, cliffy grade. While less exposed to the sea, they were more vulnerable to wind-snapped trees coming off the slope above.

Aside from the fish processing plant and company-owned store, there was a post office, a marine repair shop, a bar, a public library, a school, a cafe and gift shop, some B&Bs, and a combination laundry/steam bath/liquor store. The whole shebang ran for about a mile and then ended at a tidal flat.

People traveled mostly on foot along this winding planked thoroughfare, though some used bikes or the occasional ATV or golf cart.

In addition to the boardwalk Bellport also had one gravel road that curved up the mountain, so that the garbage truck could reach the dump.

Craving a milk shake, I walked straight to the cafe. The place was cozy, with seven red stools at a counter facing the grill and five tables positioned by the windows. I stepped in and waved hello to the one customer there. In his seventies, Uncle Bill was a wiry, handsome half-Tlingit native with twinkly brown eyes. I'm not sure why everyone called him Uncle Bill, but they did.

As soon as the waitress handed me my shake I felt better, and as soon as I took my first slurp my bad mood was cured.

"Hi, Uncle Bill," I said, sitting at the table next to him.

He adjusted his chair to face me better. After we talked about the weather—could be wetter, we agreed—he asked amiably, "How do you like living out at Steep Cove?"

Naturally he knew I was staying in the cabin. I'd personally raised the population of Bellport an entire percent! Although, if I had let that chainsaw drop an inch or two further it could have gone right back down. The thought made me want to laugh, a little hysterically. "It's more exciting than I expected," I admitted, and explained about the tree down on the beach

He said brightly, "That reminds me of a story. You ever hear about the Fields?"

Uncle Bill was going to tell me a story. My heart gave a glad little skip because I love stories, especially true ones. I told him I had not heard of the Fields.

"Yeah, Roy and Mabel Field. They lived on the same beach as you, out at Steep Cove. This was back, maybe in the fifties, before statehood, anyway." Slurping on my milk shake, I nodded happily to show I was listening. "Mabel was a mail-order bride," he continued. "She lived somewhere back east and the two of them got in touch through an ad, and she came to be with him. Roy ordered her!" Uncle Bill's face crinkled in a smile. "So the mailboat didn't come all the way out here. He had to go pick her up in Hoonah. My father—his name was Yjalmer—had a fishing boat and offered him a ride. They got to Hoonah, and Roy was napping so Yjalmer went to see when the mail boat was due. It had just come in and he saw a woman looking a little lost, so he says to her, "Are you Mabel?"

She said, "Oh, Roy!" and threw herself in his arms. When he finally got free of her, he said, "I'm Yjalmer. Roy's on the boat!"

We laughed and I thought that was the whole story, but Bill went on to say that the Fields spent many happy years at Steep Cove, but they had an incident that almost cut short their lives together.

I sat up, realizing that this was the story he'd been moving us toward.

"They came into town for something, a Christmas pageant maybe, and afterward, skiffing back home, they noticed something funny. They always left a light on at the cabin to guide them back in the dark, but their light was out. They went real slow, worried about hitting that point. You know that point; it sticks way out? They finally made it to their beach and realized why they couldn't see their light. A mudslide had come down and completely buried their home. Everything—all gone!" He took a bite of his rockfish burger and said cheerfully, "I guess one tree down on your outhaul is better than half the mountainside on your head."

Later, when I got back to Steep Cove, of course all I could think about was the steep slope looming over the cabin's back wall. It pressed so close it was impossible to even step off the back porch. You ran your nose into a cliff. A chunk of the mountain breaking off and thundering down would instantly reduce the cabin to a pile of toothpicks, and I'd just be a red smear.

An active imagination can be a burden, sometimes.

Find something relaxing to do, I ordered myself. Though the cabin didn't have many of the standard ways to relax, it did have a wonderful tub. On a previous visit I'd brought a supply of fancy sponges, candles, girly scents, and even little notebooks with lightly waxed paper that allowed me to write while soaking away. I got excited by the prospect of being warm for the first time in days, submerged in luscious bubbly scented water. Maybe that would stimulate some brilliant writing!

With no fire going in the woodstove the propane heater was supposed to kick in, but only cold water flowed from the faucet. I noticed the heater's pilot light was out and realized the wind, gusting in through the cabin cracks the other night, had probably snuffed it out.

The diagram on how to light the pilot was too faded to read. I twisted knobs this way and that, waving the lighter all over the place. After long moments of hissing and no ignition I felt like I was just begging for an explosion.

I tossed the lighter down, stomped over to the VHF, and grabbed up the radio mic. "Tom? You pick me up Tom? Channel One?"

I wanted instruction on lighting the pilot light. But also, it irked me that he hadn't called to check in. Even if he didn't think to worry about me using the chainsaw—a tree down on the beach wasn't an ordinary event—what about all the little things that could happen? How did he know I hadn't slipped and hit my head in the skiff and drowned in the rainwater collecting in the bottom? Keying the mic, I repeated, "Pick me up, Tom? Channel one? Come in?"

"Ahoy, Steep Cove." It wasn't Tom's voice I heard. It was a gravelly voice, one that sounded sea captain-ish.

"Is that you, John?" John was the kindly seventy-something neighbor Tom had told me to call if I had questions.

"Yes. Are you calling for Tom?"

"Yeah," I said.

"Oh," he said. "So you're at the cabin?"

"Yes . . . fishing's slow, so I decided to take some shore time."

"Well, do you need something?"

"No, I was just . . . trying to call him."

"Okay," John paused. "Do you want us to call his cell phone from the house phone here? Maybe we can give him a message for you."

Yes, have him call me, I yearned to say. But a message like that would prompt him to pull his gear and charge into radio range—fine if I had an emergency, but wanting a bath didn't exactly qualify. "No, that's okay."

"I see," John said. "Well, I guess, good evening out."

The ringing silence in the cabin closed around me as I hung up the radio mic. I felt a suffocating aloneness.

John's voice boomed back. "Carole, you still there?"

I pounced on the mic. "I'm here!"

"If you're not fishing, do you want a few days of work? I'm putting the *Lightly* on the grid tomorrow and could use a hand with painting."

"Work? Painting? Yes!" I noticed I was shouting jubilantly into the VHF and made myself calm down.

The grid in Bellport's harbor was a row of steel I-beams

extending perpendicular from the base of the dock. As the tide withdrew, a boat needing work settled its narrow keel across the I-beams, and there it sat, lashed to the pilings, its hull fully exposed until the tide returned.

"What time?" I asked John.

"The tide should be out by early afternoon. Why don't you come by the house around noon and have lunch with us."

"Fine, good. I'll see you then." I almost added, "Roger, wilco! Over and out, good buddy!" But I refrained.

John ended the conversation the same way he had before, with a cordial, "Good evening out."

Five

JOHN AND BETTY LIVED on the edge of Bellport in a house perched on a small, rocky rise overlooking the inlet. I moored my skiff at their dock, and with Fidget following close, ascended a ramp to their postage-stamp yard, went up some long stairs, and knocked on the door.

Betty had lunch set out already. Fidget curled up on an oval braided rug by the couch, keeping me in sight, while we women took one bench seat at the table and John folded his lanky frame onto the seat across from us. Next to my elbow sprawled *Atlantic Monthly* and *New Yorker* magazines, and above my head hung a pot of geraniums in full bloom.

I gratefully filled my plate with two grilled cheese sandwiches, a mound of applesauce, and three ginger cookies with white icing. Over lunch we made small talk and Betty called me "honey." As craggy and interesting as John's face was, hers was beautiful, framed by silver hair that swept up in soft curls. When she smiled, which happened often, the room brightened. Though I didn't know them well, I leaned into their company and found something warm and solid.

After lunch, John estimated the tide needed to go out a bit more before we could work on the boat, so he went to putter in the basement while Betty and I lingered at the kitchen table. Through a large picture window we watched salmon jumping all over the inlet. An eagle came into view. Talons extended, it swooped down to the water and back up again, making a dozen tries before catching what was most likely a humpy salmon. The fish, it looked to be about a three-pounder, flexed back and forth, fighting against the piercing talons as the eagle flew away.

Betty nudged the plate of cookies toward me and I obligingly took another. Her eyes bright, she asked, "Have you ever been real close to an eagle?"

I shook my head.

"One fall," she said, "we were with our kid Chrissie and her husband Mark, on the *Lightly*, coming back from a hunting trip. We were miles offshore and saw something struggling in the water. It was an eagle, and it was in real trouble. They can't fly if they end up wet like that."

"What do you think happened?"

She tilted her head thoughtfully. "I don't know. Maybe it was going for a fish and something distracted it?"

I could easily see the eagle getting a sudden leg cramp, or a bug in the eye. Yes, my brain works a Disney cartoon sometimes. But who knows? Maybe it did happen that way.

"Anyway," she continued, "Mark went to scoop the bird

up, making sure to wear gloves, but it didn't matter, that thing had no fight. He brought it onboard and the poor bird sat huddled in the wheelhouse doorway, keeping one eye on us while we kept one eye on him."

She smiled, "Then Mark got a bright idea and took our spotlight—you know how the bulb gets warm? Well, he shined that light on the eagle to help dry its feathers. Pretty soon the eagle noticed the warmth and turned toward the heat and started wiggling his feathers."

Betty imitated the eagle's haughtily pleased expression and rolled her slim shoulders to show me. "When we tied up at our dock he was still perched in the pilothouse doorway. Mark and John stepped right past him but Chrissie and I felt we needed to give that beak a little room." She gave a merry laugh. "So we climbed out through the pilothouse window."

"What happened to him?" I asked.

John had finished in the basement and joined us by now, so he took up the story. "Eventually he heaved up into the air, but he barely made it to the beach." He pointed to the rocky shore that lay just below their house. "He stayed there for at least a week. We tossed our deer hides onto the rocks near him—the hides have patches of very thin muscles on their underside, 'bug-twitching muscles' I call them—and that eagle sat there planing that meat off the hide with his beak, strip after strip of it. His crop got so full, he was bulging out to here." John gestured like he was holding a basketball in front of his neck.

"One day he was ready," Betty said, "and he flew away."

John glanced out the window and observed that the tide

had receded enough to let us start working on the *Lightly*. We left the house and climbed into what he called the "buggy." It was the width of a golf cart but had an enclosed cab lofty enough to accommodate his substantial height. The rear bed was like that of a pickup, but shrunk down to a miniature size. Fidget sat in the cab beside me and instead of looking outside like a regular dog, she braced her shoulder against the window, turned to me with a big-eyed "oh no" look, and stayed that way for the entire length of the boardwalk.

On the far end of the boardwalk we plunged down to the beach and ploughed to a stop in the shadow of the *Lightly*, resting on the grid. Fully out of the water, it was both gigantic and lovely, and for a moment all I could do was gawk at the majestic sight.

I sprung open the door and Fidget minced away, glad to be out of the buggy, and I climbed out after her. My boots squished into ground that had been covered by salt water just moments before, and my nose pulled in the sulfury, low-tide odor of decayed organic matter.

We unloaded gear from the back of the buggy and John assigned me the job of scraping off the barnacles, sponges, and mussels that had attached themselves to the wood hull.

He set a tall ladder under the stern, climbed to the utmost step ten feet off the mud, and began prying at a piece of ironbark. Shipwrights secure ironbark to a boat's stern or bow planks, places that need extra protection. A gap had opened up between the ironbark and the boat's stern planks and rainwater was getting in there and causing rot.

John's task was a challenging one because the ironbark was secured with big spikes that refused to let go. He drove in large wedges with a fat hammer and pried at it with a crowbar, then he drove the wedges in further. The ladder kept swaying like mad under the force of his blows. Finally, I couldn't stop worrying and went to steady it.

"When this comes off," *bam!* he swung the hammer, "I'll goop up the planks," *bam! bam!* "with some roofing compound," *bam!* "and scribe in a new piece of ironbark over the spot."

He dropped a tool now and again and I'd hand it back up to him, and finally the piece came free. He extended the old piece of wood down to me and said, "It's a type of eucalyptus. Mostly comes from Australia."

I was unprepared for its weight. "Ironbark's a good name for it."

He climbed down the ladder. "Harder than teak or mahogany. So dense it doesn't float."

I got back to scraping, and once done with that, John showed me how to use the power washer to remove the fine green slick of algae growing on the wood. I completed that task and the boat was finally ready to paint, but the tide was coming up around our rubber boots. We'd get the painting done on the next day's low tide, John said, but we'd have to hustle.

We packed up, woke Fidget from her nap on the beach mud, climbed in the buggy, and headed back to John's house. Just before we got there, a woman flagged us down and we rolled to a stop.

"Hey," Flo said, giving us both a warm grin. Flo lived at Steep Cove, about a half mile from my cabin. Her place was a large log house that she'd converted into a wilderness lodge.

"Are you looking for work once you finish painting the *Lightly*? Some guests just booked a stay and I could use a hand in the kitchen."

Tom once told me that Flo's guests came to sport fish or to take nature photos, but what they talked about when they got home was the exceptional food cooked up by Flo and her daughter Kathleen.

"Isn't Kathleen around?" I asked.

"She's busy and can't do it."

I was not a cook—very far from it. "Sorry, but if fishing picks up I'm going to help Tom, and if he doesn't need me I really should head back to Juneau . . ."

"Oh," she looked disappointed. "Kathleen's already committed to helping out on the scow so I'm scrambling to find someone."

The scow was the fish-buying barge anchored out near the grounds.

"The scow hired Kathleen? Because they're getting busier?" I asked. Additional helpers could be a sign that the fishermen, including Tom, were getting into more fish.

Flo shook her head. "She's just subbing for someone temporarily."

We chatted about the price fishermen were getting for silvers—both John and Flo were surprised it hadn't risen yet—then John made a motion to leave. Flo turned to me with a smile and asked, "You sure you can't help me at the lodge?"

I hesitated, then did what I thought was a polite wiggle out of it. "It's a nice offer, but I'm not so good in the kitchen."

"Oh, you'll do fine," she said, as though we'd agreed.

A silence fell and I didn't know what to say. Finally, I said, "Well, I guess I could try . . ."

She told me to come by in two days.

John put the buggy in gear and as we drove on a wave of regret swamped me. I've attracted a large assortment of jobs over the years. Aside from working as a journalist, I've shot video documentaries, done research at the Library of Congress, temped as a clerk in dozens of offices, and been an event organizer. I've also driven a dump truck, mowed grass, and dug graves. I've painted houses, fences, and now boats. One summer I hung drywall with a giant ex-con who jumped at loud noises. And here I was shaking in my rubber boots over the prospect of cooking at Flo's lodge? But there are just some things I'm not cut out to do. I also break out in a sweat if anybody says the word *babysit*. The one time I did babysit, we had the incident with the kitty litter. I won't go into it, but believe me—it was bad.

Back at John and Betty's house, I tried Tom's cell phone. Being needed back on the boat would be the perfect excuse, Flo would understand. But all I got was the annoying message that he was out of cell range.

I bid my new friends goodbye and returned to the damp, chilly cabin. I didn't even bother to make a fire. It was a lot of effort, I ended up all sooty, and the flames never lasted more than ten minutes anyway. I washed up, made a meal of popcorn, stirred up some hot chocolate, grabbed a blanket and crawled into the beanbag chair. The fake zebra fur was comically ugly, but it also happened to be soft and warm.

Fidget came over and gazed at me. Her brown eyes looked concerned. She even had a wrinkle on her forehead. Crunching on my dinner, I agreed with her that I was ill prepared to do this job at the lodge, but there was some good news. I was experienced, at least, in being ill prepared. It could even be called my forte.

I wasn't lying to Fidget when I made the claim. A shining example that demonstrated my knack for cluelessness was the house I bought in Juneau. I had no idea how much work the old three-story building would require, even though it was obvious in about ten different ways. There were broken windows and cracked walls. Vagrants had been living in it and had started a small fire in the living room. A plumbing valve had failed and water was running continuously into the bathtub. The furnace was sending exhaust into the house instead of out. Plus, it had the saddest, creepiest vibe imaginable—it had been a halfway house for drug and alcohol abusers in its previous life. The bedrooms had deadbolts on the doors, and pinups on the ceilings.

The housing market was sizzling hot at the time, and most properties were selling within hours. This place had been on the market, untouched, for eight months

After signing on it I talked to at least a dozen people, educated people, with money, who had looked at it and decided: no way. But so far I'd successfully juggled the gigantic mortgage and renovation costs with income and sweat equity. It was stressful, but I'd managed to stay afloat.

So if I was bold enough to take on that big bad house, cooking a little food should be a snap. That was the pep talk I tried giving the dog, and myself, that evening.

But a certain image was stuck in my head, and it refused to go away. It was one of Gary Larson's cartoons, and it captured perfectly my fears concerning the job at Flo's. The cartoon was a drawing of a kitchen freshly destroyed, as though a big bomb had just exploded, and you see a woman clad in a ruffled apron, sprawled on the floor beside a book lying face down. The book's cover said: *Recipes for Disaster*.

I wrestled with the question a while longer, but ultimately decided that I shouldn't foist my inexperience on Flo and her guests. I needed to cancel.

I called the lodge on the VHF but got no response. Going over to tell her in person was a possibility, but her place, like mine, was only reachable by boat, and I wasn't familiar with her outhaul setup. The was a good chance of tangling my prop in her line.

One more day of work with John, and then Flo expected me to start the day after. I resolved to use John and Betty's phone the following day to call Flo and warn her: She really needed to find someone else.

~~~~~

For lunch the next day Betty had prepared ramen noodle soup, with some hot dog pieces added to it. My admiration for the rhododendron blooming outside in the yard
~~~~~

prompted her to announce the big news—she had one ripe raspberry on her raspberry bush.

John, peering out the window, said, "Oh? Which one's the raspberry bush?"

She smiled demurely and said, "I don't think I'll tell you."

They both laughed, and Betty got up to serve dessert—fruit cocktail and Fig Newtons. As we started on the sweets, we heard the growl of the midday floatplane going overhead. Betty asked if I heard about the wheeled-plane pilot who, a few years before, had circled over Bellport radioing for help. It took me a second to understand she'd mentioned the plane had wheels because the water was the only place to touch down.

"What happened?"

"We heard him on the VHF asking where he could put down. Someone responded and told him we have no airstrip, but suggested the flats might work in an emergency."

I nodded. That was the only relatively flat area around, when it wasn't submerged under the tide.

"But," Betty said, "someone else spoke up, saying it was high water, and the flats were covered. And then this silence came over the radio, while everybody's thinking, *uh-oh.* It was fall, and the pilot had miscalculated on how fast it was getting dark. Small planes didn't have today's navigation equipment back then, so sight flying was it. He wasn't going to make his way through all that dark back to Juneau's airport.

"But after a minute, this fisherman came on and suggested the pilot turn and head north along the coast.

He told him to hug the shore until he saw the lights at Yakutat's airport. Even in the dark, the white of the breakers against the shore would show him the way."

"Did he make it?" I asked.

"We never heard a thing, so we knew he made it fine."

I realized she was implying that if there had been a disaster, the search would have been all over the VHF.

John and Betty chatted for a few minutes about ordering him some new wool pants, while I sat appreciating how Bellport people could turn events into stories as naturally as other people breathed the air. Like Betty's story the day before about rescuing the eagle, and now this one, about the pilot's peril. And Uncle Bill at the cafe, telling me about the landslide that buried the Field's Steep Cove cabin. It made me wonder if there was a magic blend of molecules in this Outer Coast air that infused people with a talent for sharing stories. Or perhaps it wasn't the air, but the water—people working on the ocean, traveling on it, living on stilts above it, eating food from it. Or maybe it wasn't the air or the water; perhaps when people got pummeled by nature, or by circumstances, stories were sparked.

Then I leaned back to admire the geranium blooming over my head and I thought of something that felt closer to the truth: What if stories were everywhere, and a person just had to slow down enough to hear them?

John rose from the table, glanced outside at the tide, and said, "Better get to work, I suppose."

We were already in the buggy rolling down the boardwalk when it hit me that I'd forgotten to phone Flo to get out of the cooking job. I was tempted to ask John to stop and let me use the pay phone as we flashed by it, but he was leaning forward, intent on getting to work. I made a mental note to call as soon as we quit for the day.

At the boat, John continued working on the stern and I got busy rolling on the paint. I expressed worry that the paint wouldn't dry before the tide rose, and John explained that bottom paint had a handy property: it needed to go on a dry surface but once applied, it could get wet immediately. I had once seen people dressed in chest waders who were frantically painting upward on their boat's hull, applying paint just ahead of the rising tide. Now I understood it wasn't as crazy as it had looked.

The tide was rolling in, and we had to hustle to finish our tasks. We finished but with little time to spare.

Back at John's house I used the phone to call Flo at the lodge, but got a busy signal. I hung up and heard Betty say, "Come on, you two," and realized she had set a place at the dinner table for me. I protested weakly, but she just waved me and John into our seats and ladled out three bowls of chicken soup.

After dinner I accepted John's offer to "splice the main brace." He had a whiskey while Betty and I each sipped an Irish Cream, and I sat there with my neighbors knowing it was too late to fink out on Flo. She wouldn't be able find someone else before morning.

When I left, Betty gave me a hug good-bye, and John saw me to the door.

Back inside the chilly cabin I pulled a comforter around

my shoulders and watched the light fade from the day. I'd made some cash, which felt good, but the prospect of cooking at the lodge the next day made my stomach ache. It was a mistake for me to hire on as a cook, especially at a lodge with a reputation for excellent eats.

The VHF crackled, reminding me to try Tom again, and this time he came back to the call, but unfortunately our signal kept cutting in and out. Glad for even this scratchy contact, I asked how it was going, hoping to hear him say the word "backhoe."

But he just said things were okay, and asked how the firewood supply was holding out. I confessed that I couldn't keep a fire going and he came back to say my response had just come through as static, but he hoped I was staying warm enough. My attempt to ask about the pilot light on the water heater met with a similar lack of success, and my agitation climbed as we threw words across the span and missed. Finally, without even a decent goodbye, or any kind of goodbye, I gave up and put the radio mic down, feeling literally, as well as figuratively, cut off.

A fisherman called on the VHF a moment later and offered to relay a message. His signal was almost as weak, but I was grateful to get my chance, at least, to say something like goodbye. I said, "Please—tell—Tom—I'll—talk—to—him—um . . . really—soon, I hope."

Six

THE NEXT MORNING, I circled the skiff in front of Flo's place. She ambled down the path, a hand raised in welcome. Realizing my concern about tangling in her outhaul, she waved her arms, directing me toward a safe landing.

Flo was in her mid-fifties, tan and athletic with brown eyes that shone with an alert warmth. While we secured my skiff to her outhaul, she told me the welcome news that Kathleen wasn't due on the fish-buying scow until the following morning, so we'd overlap for my first day.

Willowy and green-eyed, Kathleen greeted me with a ready smile, and we got to work preparing the guest rooms.

When the state ferry steamed by and threw its heavy wake on the beach, she took the skiff to Bellport to pick up the arriving guests and to buy some broccoli to round out the dinner menu.

An hour later she returned with the guests. Nosing the skiff up to the beach, she hopped out to place a plastic step stool in the surf's edge. We stood on either side in our rubber boots, offering a hand as the two women and then the two men each climbed onto the stool, and then took a giant step to reach the dry beach rocks.

Kathleen put the skiff on the outhaul while I lugged a cart of baggage up a gravel path to the lodge. The guests followed along behind, brushing through wild asters and lilies, and pausing to pick from the heavily laden blueberry bushes. Everyone gathered at the top of the path to marvel over a weathered, thigh-high whale vertebra resting in the grass near the lodge entrance.

After sorting themselves out, three of the guests went sport fishing with Flo's grown son Dennis while the fourth guest stayed behind, wanting to read by the fire.

Flo, Kathleen, and I went into a flurry of dinner preparations. The menu included thick fillets of grilled king salmon, homemade bread, dinner salad with sliced avocado, and a broccoli-cheese bake.

Kathleen suddenly clapped her hand to her mouth and looked at her mother with round eyes. "I forgot to buy broccoli in town."

"Ah, don't sweat the small stuff," Flo said. Turning to me, she added with a shrug, "It's all small stuff."

I was familiar with the expression but was never more relieved to hear it. If Flo went by this philosophy it suddenly seemed possible that we might survive my presence in the kitchen—and maybe even end up friends.

To replace broccoli on the menu Flo directed Kathleen and me to get some goose tongue from the beach. As we filled our bowls with the succulent beach greens,

Kathleen told me, “We’ll sauté it with bacon and onions. We need to pick a lot because people always want seconds.”

We got back to the lodge and the guest sitting by the fire rose and came over, looking distressed. “What’s in that bowl?” he asked.

Kathleen tipped her bowl to show him the pointed strands, which really were shaped like a goose’s tongue. “It’s a beach green called goose tongue.”

“Oh.” He relaxed. “I thought you went to the beach to get ‘goose dung.’”

~~~~~

Dear Mary,

I found some work cooking at my neighbor’s wilderness lodge. Me—cooking! Shocker, I know.

Today I was assigned to make the pecan pie. As it was my first pie ever, I started well before dinner and followed the recipe closely. But the piecrust was giving me a bunch of trouble. I tried to roll it out but it kept tearing. I hid in the kitchen, mauling that poor dough, while everyone gathered in the main room for dinner.

“C’mon and eat,” my boss Flo urged me from where she sat at the table, assuming the pie was in the oven and I was just putting things away. “I’ll be just a sec,” I said in my cheeriest voice. “Go ahead and start!”

But they wanted to wait for me. So I went ahead and laid my fingerprinty crust into the bottom of the pie plate—it didn’t even come halfway up the sides. Feeling desperate, I globbed in the filling and with a wince, laid my little mutant crust on top. And that was when it dawned on me—pecan pie has no top crust!

Right at that moment, Flo popped into the kitchen.
~~~~~

She looked at the pie and back at me, and we started laughing. Of course everybody jumped up from the table and crowded into the kitchen to see my pecan pie wearing that top crust like a dented beanie.

We went ahead and baked the pie like that and when it came time for dessert we all kept laughing at the sight. I guess if you count the glee factor, it was a highly successful pie.

Okay, sis, it's past my bedtime, so I'll say goodnight.

Carole

xxoo

The next morning my shift started at six. To get my skiff from its outhaul, I had a walk of a hundred yards down the rocky, kelp-strewn beach. I threw a stick for the dog and stopped a couple of times, just to breathe in the air. It tasted of something sweet and oceany, and made me think of porpoise smiles and, strangely enough, spanikopita.

I hauled on the line to bring in the skiff, but to my dismay the rope came in and clotheslined back out, while the skiff stayed where it was. To secure the skiff's bowline to the outhaul line I'd invented my own special knot, a series of elaborate twists and loops. Unfortunately, earnestness isn't enough to make a knot hold, so it had come uncinched. I could pull the outhaul line until I turned purple, but the skiff wasn't going to come in with it.

I went and got a towel, and reluctantly stripped and swam out to the skiff. Puffing and gasping in the fifty-degree water, I towed it back to the beach. Wide awake now, and shivery, I toweled off, pulled on my clothes and got to the lodge only a few minutes late.

Flo was hunkered on a little stool in front of the open woodstove, just starting her wood fire. I plunked down on the floor next to her, determined to study her every move.

As a kid I went to Girl Scouts on my first day, all excited, thinking *camping, canoeing, survival games in the woods*... but the troop's activities were mainly crafts, not outdoorsy things. Glitter and glue, fabric, ribbon, and yarn—these things happen to stress me out. It could be part of the same nervous condition I get around babies and, until recently, kitchens. I tried valiantly to be a Girl Scout, but after two hours, I threw up and had to go home.

Flo arranged a pile of crumpled newspaper, laid a few sticks of kindling over the paper, and patiently fed the licking flames with pieces of wood. She toyed with the draft, adding air to fan the flames and backing it off when the flames faltered from too much draft. I saw the way she built the fire, bit by bit, and was inspired to get my own woodstove going that evening.

We made everyone breakfast and sent the guests off with bag lunches to go fly-fishing with Dennis. After cleaning up the kitchen, Flo and I got busy picking berries.

The thick stands of berry bushes surrounding the lodge were dripping with fruit—blueberries, raspberries, huckleberries, strawberries, and salmonberries. We hung our buckets on strings around our necks so we had our hands hung free to pick, and fell into a rhythm of easy silences broken up with bits of conversation.

Over the next couple of hours I learned that Flo grew up in the nearby town of Sitka where she taught physical education and girls' health to high schoolers. I also learned that she was a pilot in the Sitka Flying Club in her twenties.

"Were there many women in the club?" I asked.

"Just me," she said with a laugh.

After she married and started a family, they made their living fishing for salmon.

"So you liked fishing?" I said.

"Oh yeah," she said. "But parts of it were hard. I had to suppress my independence, you know, take orders. I liked it fine for fifteen years, but one day I woke up to the fact that there were other jobs I could do on the beach to make money."

"Like what?"

"A friend and I got the contract to paint the school buildings, so for one summer I worked on that, around the weather. I loved it—got a Walkman and painted away. And now, of course, I have the lodge and the magistrate job."

I asked about the type of crimes she encountered working as the district judge, but she answered vaguely, and I realized she either couldn't or wouldn't discuss it.

Her voice floated over to me from the middle of a thick web of blueberry bushes. "So where did you live before Juneau?"

I popped a berry into my mouth. "I tried out a couple of different cities. I lived in Washington, D.C., but I didn't really fit in there."

"How come?"

"Every place has its culture, right?" I could see her

looking over at me, listening as she picked. "In D.C., I'd meet someone and they'd immediately ask, 'So . . . what do you do?' The question always felt more like, 'So . . . what can you do for me? Or against me?'" I saw a fat berry hiding under a leaf and picked it. "I worked for *Common Cause* magazine but when folks asked what I did, even though they meant for work, I told them I played ultimate Frisbee."

"Did you?" Flo laughed.

"Not very well," I laughed with her. "I was just trying to find someone who could step outside the box, conversation-wise."

"Did it work?"

"Nah," I said, and we laughed again.

We picked a while and then she asked, "Where else did you live?"

"I lived in San Francisco, and there it was play, play, play. Nobody brought up the subject of work." I shrugged. "I couldn't jive with people being so California-happy all the time. I need to be around a certain amount of suffering, being from the Midwest." Flo was laughing again. "So then I moved to Chicago and it was a perfect fit. I loved Chicago."

"So what made you leave?"

She'd make a good reporter, I thought.

"Oh, I started to feel crazy busy," I replied, "and wanted to get off the hamster wheel."

Putting it that way made it sound a lot less impulsive, less shocking, than it actually was. One day I noticed life had become awfully hectic, but instead of ignoring it like a normal person would, I started yearning for that more leisurely pace found out West. On an impulse,

I sent my résumé to editors heading up newspapers and magazines in places like Albuquerque, Denver, Phoenix, Sacramento, Portland, and Seattle. On a whim—call it an impulse within an impulse—I included Alaska's three largest cities: Anchorage, Fairbanks, and Juneau.

To my surprise the editor of Juneau's newspaper responded with an offer to fly me to Alaska for a one-day "working" interview.

On the morning of the big day, the editor, Larry, explained I was to conduct interviews for two different stories and write one of them up by afternoon. Then he handed me the keys to his new Volvo and pointed me downtown for my first interview.

Juneau's downtown is sometimes called "Little San Francisco" for its steep streets, quaint waterfront, and many tourists. The subject of the story was Juneau's first bicycle-cab business. A guy nicknamed "Herky" was hauling visitors around in an open hackney while telling them local lore.

I wedged Larry's Volvo in an impossibly small spot on a hill, turned the wheels to the curb, and sat wondering how I'd pull this interview off. Larry had said, "Just look for the pedicab; he's the only one."

Sure enough, because the downtown is small, after walking only a few blocks I caught sight of the guy crossing an intersection a block away. What followed resembled one of those Three Stooges chase scenes in a maze of hallways—except it was a maze of streets, and there was only one stooge.

I'd stupidly overdressed in a silk pencil skirt that hindered even a normal walking stride. I took off after him, using rapid, little skipping steps and caught up with him only because he had three Japanese tourists and their mountain of baggage in his cab, and he was going up a steep hill.

"Hi, I'm Carole," I puffed, skipping alongside, "with the newspaper. Can I interview you for a story?" I heard these little ripping sounds and realized the slit on my skirt was inching higher up my leg.

He grinned at me and said, "Sure, meet me at the Armadillo."

"When?"

"Half hour," he said.

The Armadillo turned out to be a fabulous Mexican restaurant, and when Herky showed up he gave me a great interview. He was full of wisecracks and enthusiasm. For life, for his business, for the plate of enchiladas in front of him, for pretty much everything. He had started the business so that he could do something physical all summer, then take winters off to do what he loved, which was ski. The concept of structuring one's life seasonally was foreign to me. By the end of the interview, which went for hours, my face hurt from laughing and I had pretty much decided I was moving to Juneau—whether I got the job or not.

Because Herky's story promised to be a long and entertaining piece, I couldn't bear the thought of hacking it together in just an afternoon. So I decided the story I'd write up and give to Larry at the end of the day would be the second interview he'd assigned me, a profile of a priest who was new to town.

In profiling people, I'd found that even shy people, or those who are grumpy, actually enjoy talking if they are asked the right question. To this day, I still don't know what the right question might be with regard to that priest. I've never met anyone so resolutely dull. I wasn't convinced he even had a pulse.

I frantically tried to inject some zest into that article. I called people in his former parish, but nobody could think of anything to say other than, "Uh . . . yeah, he was our priest . . ."

When I emailed the article to Larry, I knew it was DOA.

He called me into his office. "There are problems with this story," he said.

I winced and said, "I know."

He was looking at the screen and shaking his head in bewilderment. "Your writing samples are good, great even." Before I could decide how to respond, he leaned back, his eyes still on the screen, and said, "You seem confident you can do this job."

"Absolutely." I said this with all my heart.

He finally looked at me, and it was one of those close looks, where you know a person is thoroughly reading you.

I held his gaze, thinking, *hire me, hire me, hire me.*

"I don't know why . . ." he paused, "but I'm going to hire you."

I grinned and said, "I'm glad."

He said dryly, "Let's hope I am, too."

He gave me two weeks to go back to Chicago, say my good-byes, and return for good. He also wanted me to write up the Herky story and send it to him. Later, he confessed he read it with a profound sigh of relief because it resembled my sample clips, and not the priest story.

My assignments at the Juneau paper mostly involved profiling eccentric Alaskans. From day one, it was a blast. And for such a small place—its population was thirty thousand—I found Juneau to be fantastically fertile ground, professionally and culturally. Life was plenty exciting without being hectic. All indicators pointed to a happy future, one I anticipated sharing with some nice, respectable Juneau man.

Then I went and fell for a fisherman from Bellport.

I heard a snort, and looked up from picking huckleberries to see a sea lion's head slicing the water like a wedge. Daylight slicked along his blubbery back as he arched and dove out of sight.

Yikes, I thought, I *really* got off that hamster wheel.

SEVEN

WE PICKED BERRIES until it was time to eat lunch, and after lunch we sipped coffee by the fire. Rough job, I know.

When she heard about my chilly swim that morning, Flo went in the storage room and returned with two lengths of rope. "Okay," she said, handing me one rope. "Make a loop like this. Now, here's where the rabbit pops up through the hole, runs around the tree, and goes back down the hole." Tom had shown me this and I could never seem to get it. But like me Flo was left-handed, so I was able to follow her example. Suddenly the rabbit, the hole, the tree, they all made sense to me. We did it a few times until I had the bowline down.

Knot-tying, fire-building, berry picking, chitchatting—what a great day this was turning out to be. And the best was yet to come.

That night we made a venison stir-fry for dinner. I hadn't consumed wild meat before but had heard it described as gamey-tasting. Just the word "gamey" made my stomach twist, so I didn't expect to like it.

So it stunned me, the way venison tasted. It was flavorful and complex without being in the least "strong." Aside from the gorgeous flavor, each bite seemed to send a liveliness humming through my body. It reminded me of the feeling I had when eating wild fish.

I marveled about it to Flo and she said, "Venison energy." She said it matter-of-factly, but her eyes were bright. "Try that piece." She pointed to a small morsel on my plate. "See what you think."

It was more dense than the rest, and juicier. I found the flavor intense, but beautifully so. "What is it?"

"You like it?"

"I love it."

"That's heart," she nodded. "Everybody loves it."

~~~~~

After dinner I used the phone at the lodge to try calling Tom. His cell phone on the boat didn't always work, but I was in luck. He answered, but warned me he was rounding a point and was going to lose his signal, so we needed to talk fast.

He reported that the fishing had improved to where it was nice and steady, but he'd had no big days yet. We discussed whether it was worthwhile for me to stick around. Fishing could get super busy any day, he said, and it would pay if I wanted to fish some more. I said I'd stay a bit longer to see what happened and told him I needed advice on how to light the pilot on the water heater.

He walked me through the steps and then asked how
~~~~~

everything was going. I told him how I'd taken work with Flo and he said, "That's great!"

I had so many things I wanted to tell him. There was my budding friendship with John and Betty and my scary chainsaw experience, and what a sweetheart Fidget was, and I wanted to ask if he'd heard Uncle Bill's story about the Field's mudslide.

Plus, there was the jinx thing. It wasn't a big deal—just a niggling question on my mind—but I wanted to ask if he thought the fishing got better because I'd left the boat.

I began by telling him the most recent news—that I'd fallen in love with venison, but before I even finished with that our call was cut off.

I loitered by the phone, hoping he'd turn around to regain his signal so we could talk some more. But I ended up just standing around, forlorn, as the phone stayed silent.

Suddenly Flo zoomed into the kitchen, a gaggle of guests in her wake. She grabbed a bottle of her homemade berry wine from the cupboard and wrestled free the cork. Someone cracked a joke and she threw back her head and laughed. Her laugh, a wonderful, contagious honk, sailed across the room like one of those bright orange rings you see on boats. A life-preserver in the shape of a laugh. Flo caught my eye, held out a glass of wine, and reeled me straight into the fun.

After the party wound down, I went back to the cabin and crawled up into the loft, drowsy from wine and laughter, thinking about how mirth is one of those things that heats us up from inside, a gift we can give to one another.

Then I thought about how Tom's absence and the absence of a steady job were two downers that actually had an upside. My sense of security was less, but it created an opening, a space where interesting things could happen.

~~~~~

The following morning the guests opted to sleep in, which freed Dennis, Flo's son, from his job as their fishing guide. He decided to go hunting and invited me along.

Part of me wanted to, while another part didn't. Guns scared me. Plus, the idea of witnessing the death of a deer made me tremble. But venison was an extraordinary food, and it seemed to demand more than just blind consumption from me. So I went with him.

It was six-thirty, and bright daylight when we left the lodge and skiffed to a promising creek cut. To keep the receding tide from stranding the skiff, and us, on the beach, he rigged a makeshift outhaul, and then we started climbing.

He told me that as he was growing up his family subsisted on about ten deer a year. "My dad carved us each a fake gun. Kathleen and I were about six or seven years old and we roamed for miles with him carrying those sticks. If we accidentally handled our stick wrong, pointed them anywhere near another person, we were in big trouble."

I followed Dennis up through thick forest, and after the trees petered out, we continued, scrambling upward. Interspersed among the hard, gray granite peaks were meadows lush with fragrant heather and alpine shrubs.
~~~~~

We came across a few hollows still holding snow and felt encouraged by the sight of fresh tracks. Dennis stopped often to scan the nearby rises, using the spotting scope on his rifle, and it wasn't long before he spotted a buck about two hundred yards away.

When the shot sounded I broke out in a cold sweat, overwhelmed by my fear of guns, and anxiety for the deer. A microsecond later, when the animal dropped, sadness hit me, but mingled with it came another feeling—a rush of happiness that we'd been blessed with this meat.

It was a paradox, one I doubted I would resolve easily. But if nothing else, putting myself close to the paradox and feeling these conflicted emotions seemed like the right thing to do.

Dennis began field-dressing the deer. He made several quick cuts with his knife and pulled out a huge pile of guts. To my surprise everything was packaged in a way that was relatively tidy, like with fish but on a much larger scale.

Pointing to the antlers, Dennis told me deer in Southeast Alaska were hunted for meat, not for trophies. The buck was full grown, but its antlers were under twelve inches and forked into only two small tines.

He seemed quietly grateful for the meat. His movements were calm as he wiped his knife on the moss at our feet, tied the deer's legs together, and then heaved it on like a backpack. I asked how much it weighed and he said, with the hide still on, maybe 110 or 120 pounds.

He had me carry the heart and liver inside my pack, secured in a ziplock bag. As we slipped, hopped, and crashed our way down the steep terrain, I could feel the warmth of these organs against my spine, and the intimacy of that heat brought home to me what a solemn privilege it was to eat this food. I could feel my desire for it move to a deeper, more respectful place in me.

Back at the lodge Dennis hung the deer on the back porch, and deftly skinned it and carved it into pieces. I helped Flo wrap the meat in plastic, then in white butcher paper. We labeled it with the date and whether the hunks were chops, roasts, steaks, or stew scraps. We had perhaps forty pounds of meat total and it was all in the freezer, ready to eat, before noon.

~~~~~

Dear Mary,

I am back at the cabin, sitting in the chair by the window, having just finished my week at Flo's lodge. There's bread baking in the oven and it's making the cabin smell like heaven. Ha! That's not a sentence I ever expected to write, unless composing fiction.

Here's another one: I built a sweet little fire that is giving off warmth and making a happy crackle.

In just one short week, Flo showed me how to do these things, and more. I made halibut enchiladas, baked salmon, rosemary potatoes, overnight soufflé, fish chowder, venison shish kebabs, beer-battered salmon, and rice that was not only edible, but fluffy! I learned not to fear herbs, and to trust sourdough starter. And with all my heart, I do solemnly believe that if fish is fresh-caught, a marinade has to be extraordinary or it is a crime.

I didn't become a great cook—but I was inspired by one.
~~~~~

The job involved some outdoor fun, too. I picked berries with Flo, went hunting with Dennis, and one afternoon Flo let me tag along as "assistant guide" while she led the guests into the hills behind the lodge.

There are no people-trails, just faint, winding game trails, so it was less like hiking and more like bushwhacking.

Flo brought her rifle and every few minutes cut loose with one of her bear whoops, "Whooooo Whoooop! Whoa bear!" I'd heard the advice before: make lots of noise to scare away the bears, but Flo was the first person I encountered who really let out with some serious hollering.

Apparently this island has more grizzlies than people, so to my mind, hollering seems like an excellent idea. I imitated her whoop a few times and it felt good. The guests took it in stride, figuring I was a veteran whooper. Come to think of it, I probably over-whooped on that hike, but no harm done.

Funny how much I dreaded taking this job at first.

My take-home lesson? Doing something scary can pay high dividends.

Ah, the oven timer just went off. It's time to check on my bread. You tap the loaves on their pretty brown heads and if they make this hollow bread-done sound, you know it's time to get the butter out.

Let's hear it for dividends you can eat!

Smooch your boys for me.

xxoo

Carole

~~~~~

I stayed close to the VHF hoping that Tom would call, but he did not. I kept imagining the radio crackling with his voice: "*Backhoe! Backhoe! Backhoe! Pick me up, Carole? Channel one? Where are you? I need you, the world's greatest deckhand. Get out here, quick. We're in the money now!*"

Downtime is one of my favorite things—I do it well—but to enjoy it, I need to earn it. So, instead of relishing the glorious minutes unfurling slowly one by one, I felt restless and weighed down by guilt.

This quote in a magazine caught my eye:

"Everyone needs to work. Even a lion cannot sleep, expecting a deer to enter his mouth." —Hitopadesha

I had no idea who—or what—Hitopadesha was, but found myself agreeing wholeheartedly with him, or her, or it. The cabin had no Internet so I couldn't look it up, but John and Betty were both avid readers, and their house was crammed with books. I called their house on the VHF to see if they could tell me.

Betty came back to my hail, and told me that John had taken the *Lightly* out trolling. I asked if she liked being on her own and she confessed that although she missed him, she did like eating green beans to her heart's content—she loved them, and he did not.

We laughed about that, and then I told her about the quote and asked if she knew anything about Hitopadesha.

She had me spell it for her so she could write it down, and said, "It's a Sanskrit text, I think, but hold on a minute,
~~~~~

I have a book here that will tell us." There was a clunk and a pause, and then another clunk, and she came back, saying, "It's a twelfth-century collection of Sanskrit fables and verse. It says here that it uses animals and birds to teach moral lessons and responsible statesmanship."

"You're amazing," I said.

"Once a librarian, always a librarian," she said, and gave a happy laugh.

This pleasure in Betty's voice was unmistakable. She was now retired, but had served as the town librarian for decades. I could see how it must have suited her and that she probably missed it.

Being very grounded in this life, I don't often contemplate an afterlife, but suddenly I wondered if heaven might just a place where we all get to do what we love doing, and things like money, or aging concerns just get swept aside by angel wings.

I asked Betty where she'd trained as a librarian and she said she hadn't: she became Bellport's librarian because no one else was available. "Everybody wears different hats around here," she said. "I was also the town weatherman!"

"Really? What did you do as the town weatherman?"

"In smaller towns the Weather Bureau has a person record the temperature and precipitation every day, and report it to them. I did that for seven years."

We chatted a while longer and I was grateful for the pleasant interaction, but after we signed off, I paced around, getting more and more fidgety, while the dog—despite her name—sprawled on the floor, looking extremely relaxed.

Finally, I couldn't take it anymore and went to sit beside her on the rug. I lifted her paw and studied how it hung limp in my palm, heavy with relaxation. I released it gently and lay down facing her. We curled toward each other like two apostrophes. "I must produce," I said in a monotone.

She just looked at me with trusting eyes. Their shiny, uncomplicated calm made me wish I could adopt her outlook on life. I scooched my face closer.

"This won't hurt a bit," I said, and pressed my forehead to hers. "Brain transfer," I intoned in a grave voice. I could feel her eyelids flickering, but she remained very still for the procedure.

I pulled away a few inches and said in a soft voice, "Now you can worry about being productive, and I'll just relax, okay?"

She went back to sleep, which told me the brain transfer didn't take, but some of her sweet calm did rub off on me. At least I was able to look out the window and stop fussing for a bit.

The mountains on the opposite shore of the inlet had three distinct parts. Up high, granite peaks arched skyward, kissing the clouds. Below that, deep green slopes plunged to the water's edge. And the last section of slope, invisible to the eye, continued below the water's surface, tumbling another six hundred feet before hitting the pinnacled bottom of the inlet.

I closed my eyes, picturing the little minnow-like fish that hung out down among those pinnacles, and the bigger fish that came along to eat them, and then, coming to eat those bigger fish, the monster fish of all—the halibut.

A halibut is born with a regular fish-shaped body, but as it grows, it flattens out, and strangely enough, its left eye migrates across its head until both eyes end up on the same side. So, when grown, this flat-bodied fish swims down along the bottom with both eyes peering from its top side. To better watch for food, I suppose. The migrating eye, though, doesn't quite line up with the other, which is why halibut have that goofy, skewed look to them.

One of my goals was to catch one someday. They grow to two, three, even four hundred pounds, and the idea I might catch something so delicious, and so potentially huge thrilled me. But the idea scared me, too. You pull something that big out of the ocean, and put it in a boat with you, trouble can happen. There were stories about these powerful fish thrashing around and breaking fishermen's legs against boat bulwarks. There were stories of fishermen who shot halibut in the head first before bringing them on board, just to be safe. There was also the story about the fisherman who emptied his pistol to subdue the big fish *after* bringing it on board. Talk about a bad idea.

Darkness was falling on the cabin, and I got up to light the propane lamp, still thinking about halibut. The lamp was mounted on the wall over the chair. I had to reach up to twist the valve while flicking the lighter close—but not too close—to the mantle. These mantles were delicate, and the slightest touch collapsed them into tiny ash particles. They were made of radioactive something or other, and Tom had warned me if a mantle should collapse, I must not let the particles touch me, and, never, ever, inhale them.

The gas didn't catch immediately, so I held the valve open, and the lighter steady. Then it caught. A huge flame flared out. I yanked my hand away, and grazed the mantle with my thumb. A big poof of ash rained down on me.

I stumbled to the door and ran outside, spitting and coughing and cussing.

When I finally went back in, Fidget had disappeared. My swearing had sent her dashing off to hide in the bathroom. I thought raisins might coax her out. I knew she had a thing for them, and sure enough she came out of the bathroom to take them delicately from my fingertips, one at a time.

I promised that there'd be no more swearing (that night). "I swear," I told her solemnly.

The mantle had to be replaced but I could not handle the idea of poking into dark, spidery corners to look for Tom's replacement stash. It would have to wait until my next can-do day.

I flopped into the beanbag chair and picked up my book, but just stared at the page, unseeing. I thought of a litany of things missing from my life. I missed bright lights that turned on and off with a switch. I missed watching movies, and calling up a friend to talk. I felt a sudden craving for Thai food, live music, and my car. What I missed most about my car, aside from the fact that it kept the rain off my head, was the ease with which I could park the thing. Most of all, I missed my house, and the satisfaction of checking things off my remodel to-do list.

It's time to go, came the sudden thought. I'd had enough

of this strange environment, with its lamps raining deadly dust on me. I yearned to feel productive—not radioactive. The solution was simple: In the morning, I'd go into Bellport and arrange my flight home.

I made myself a nest of blankets in the beanbag chair. Though not all that comfortable, sleeping in the front room by the window meant I'd wake up and see the water when I first opened my eyes. The view overlooking the inlet was one thing about this place, I realized, that I would dearly miss.

Eight

W*hat a soft and lovely morning,* I thought when I opened my eyes. On the inlet's glassy surface some very big brush had painted a shimmering reflection of mountains and sky, and had tinged it with the pink and orange of dawn.

By the time I'd finished my first cup of coffee, my resolve to leave had started dissolving, like the pink hue on the water.

Suspecting that I could use economics to justify staying, I did a mental tally of what I had spent while at the cabin, and it did actually amount to very little. Meals had come off the shelf at the cabin, or were taken with John and Betty, or at Flo's lodge. Propane for cooking and lights probably came to about fifty cents a day, and I'd only spent a few bucks on generator and skiff gas.

By contrast, living in Juneau was expensive. The house remodel always took plenty, but so did entertainment, food, gas for my car, utilities, plus my phone and Internet needs. Living in Juneau, I careened through cash.

So the upshot was, the income from renting out my

house took care of my usual bills, and thanks to this cabin, I wasn't burning through much money. If I stayed, I might go back out fishing and even end the summer with a savings. With only five weeks remaining in the season, deckhanding no longer held its original promise, but some potential remained.

I made a plan: I'd stay, but only give it one more week. It was Friday, and if Tom didn't tell me "backhoe" by next Friday, I would head back to Juneau. That would be my cutoff. I happily stared out the window, drinking coffee, lulled by the knowledge that a plan was in place.

A while later, into my head bobbed the image of a big, cartoonish, cross-eyed halibut. It wore a la-la-la expression and was snuffling along the ocean floor, looking for something to eat. I imagined myself in the skiff above, dropping a hook and line into the water, *plop!* I saw the halibut eat my juicy bait, *gobble, gobble*. I hauled my gigantic prize quickly to the surface, and *kerplunk!* flipped it into the skiff. Oh victorious me!

It would be so cool to catch one, I thought. With halibut, because they were so big you could freeze a bunch, but also it was customary to bring some around to your friends. I imagined how Betty's face would light up if I brought her some fresh halibut.

What a concept: I could go out the door and maybe catch a halibut, gaining food for myself plus some to share. I liked the idea. It wasn't a promise that I'd get results, like when I worked for money, but it was a way to be productive, a type of employment that had a twist to it.

I threw on some warm clothes and went in search of a halibut pole. They're sport poles, but thick as a thumb all the way to the tip. I found one in the shed, but it was loaded with monofilament that looked decades old, and its reel appeared broken.

People also fished with hand lines, I remembered, and found some of that on the porch in good shape. I put the line into a crumpled laundry basket I discovered in the shed, along with hooks and sinker weights, plus a knife.

I skiffed across the inlet, with Fidget riding shotgun. You usually see dogs facing forward, sniffing the air, tails wagging, but not her. She huddled as close to me as possible, her eyes glued to my face as though monitoring my expression to make sure the world was intact. It made me laugh, which made her grin back tentatively. Or maybe it was nervous panting. I patted her head and assured her that our world was even better than intact—it was expanding.

Needing bait, I stopped at a creek to collect a humpy salmon, selecting one that was dead, but not rotten, and then went to drift over a spot that looked inviting. I dropped my hand line down a couple hundred feet, looped the end around a brace in the skiff, and pulled out my book to read. Every once in a while I bounced my bait on the ocean floor in a way I hoped was enticing.

Raised near Detroit, I grew up far removed from people who fished or hunted, but even so, Huck Finn–like adventures dominated my young imagination. "Hey," I announced to Fidget, who was curled up on the bottom of the skiff. "I'm getting in touch with my inner Huck Finn."

She looked at me and thumped her tail twice, like she understood. Then she kept looking at me and it dawned on me she could probably use some raisins. I obliged her, then resumed reading.

The first hour yielded an exceptionally large purple starfish. I counted twenty-one legs. An hour later, up came a brown bulgy-eyed rockfish—people called them brown bombers. And right after that, I hooked a bright orange fish, called a yellow eye. I kept both the bomber and the yellow eye, because I knew they were good eating.

The fish, flopping around in the bottom of the skiff, scared Fidget. They were dinky, maybe two or three pounds each, but she moved as far from them as possible and stood, shivering anxiously. I tried not to think about how she would react when I hauled my big halibut into the skiff with us.

Moving into deeper water, I bounced my weight on the bottom and got a large tug on the line. I pulled like crazy, hand over hand, excited by the weight on the end of the line. But instead of my dream halibut, what broke the surface was a prehistoric-looking creature, rolling bleak yellow eyes and flashing a spooky overbite at me. It was about four feet long, with an undulating, diamond-shaped body. I cut the line quick, and it snapped its teeth at me, rolled its cape-like wings, and disappeared into the depths.

My heart was still galloping from this when I saw a squall charging across the inlet toward me, whipping up the water, thickening the air with rain.

I gripped the sides of the skiff anxiously, but the squall

just made things bouncy and wet for about sixty seconds and then blew by.

I had to laugh, because my reaction was just like Fidget's fear of the snappers. It sprang from nervous not-knowing. An uncomfortable thing, not-knowing, but it passes, like the squall, and then you know.

An hour later the air temperature took a dive, so I quit and went back to the cabin. I got busy right away and filleted my bomber and yellow eye. Actually, because Tom had always performed this task, I didn't fillet them so much as mangle them. I also stabbed both my thumbs on the snappers' dorsal spines, which stuck up like fat needles. But I didn't care. I ate every scrap of the day's catch and it tasted tremendous.

Afterward I gave Fidget the fish skin, slathered antiseptic on my throbbing thumbs, and sat down with a cup of coffee to think. An odd little thrill kept tickling my insides, and it had to do with catching and eating those fish.

Dear Mary,

Here on this Outer Coast people pursue what's called a subsistence lifestyle. It's a fancy way of saying they live off wild stuff like fish and deer and berries. (You would too if you saw what little was in the store.)

So today, I just caught my own lunch, and I'm sitting here feeling this satisfied glow inside. A full stomach but more than that somehow.

This day has stirred up an old memory. Do you remember that patch of woods across the street from our house? When I was ten, I dragged an old wood pallet into a mud hole over there, and for an entire summer played like I was Huck Finn. I traveled a river in my mind, overcoming hazards and having adventures.

I paused, knowing Mary would laugh as she read this. I was a nervous, skinny kid who cried at the least provocation. How could she not be amused to hear I'd dreamed up this alternate world, where my awkward, shy self could be the bold adventurer.

So, sis, did any particular activity make you happy as a kid? Have you ever noticed some kids get an entranced look on their faces when doing various things? Like drawing, or building with blocks, dressing up dolls, or kicking a ball. It's interesting, the way we all gravitate toward certain things.

I'm starting to think that even if we let go of our first passions, maybe they never let go of us. I forgot about this girl-child I used to be, playing in the woods. But it's like she never stopped existing; she just curled up deep inside me and took a long nap. But she's awake now.

And that special satisfaction I feel today, this weird happiness in me? It's like I'm being reunited with someone I was once close to.

Okay, enough navel-gazing. The fire's dying down; I'd better go feed it.

Hugs to everyone.

xxoo

Carole

I started to get up, but paused to tack on an additional thought.

PS: Oh-oh. Remember that rocking horse we had? I spent a crazy amount of time on that thing, staring off

> into space, having cowboy dreams. (Not *those* kind—they came later.) So does this mean I'm also a cowpoke inside, too?
>
> And all those hours spent bouncing on the pogo stick? What does *that* signify?

Smiling, I closed my notebook and went to stoke the fire.

~~~~~

While making their run into freshwater to spawn, salmon stop eating, even though some will need to journey hundreds of miles before they get to their original spawning grounds. So, those last weeks on the ocean, before entering the inland waters, they eat like crazy, fattening up for the run. This makes them more inclined to strike at a fisherman's lure, but also, as they grow fatter, they become worth more. Silvers caught in the beginning of the season average about three pounds, whereas by mid-August, they weigh at least double that. The same number of fish, but twice the weight, which means twice the money. And, their size keeps climbing upward on this steep curve until the fishing season closed at the end of September.

This was the first reason fishermen could always count on increased revenues as the season progresses. The second reason was that the price buyers paid fishermen always increased over the course of the summer, often significantly. Buyers hadn't hiked the price yet this summer, which was odd, but at least the fish were fattening up nicely, and it was widely anticipated that the price would take a jump soon, probably a big one.
~~~~~

After throwing a stick on the beach for Fidget, I stepped into the cabin and heard a couple of fishermen on the VHF talking about price. I couldn't catch much of what they said due to a poor signal, but started to wonder if they were just gabbing, or if there had been a price increase. Hoping to find out and wishing to get in a chat with Tom, I went to town and called him from the payphone outside the post office.

He answered and told me his cell signal was strong, and the fishing was slow. A good time to talk, he said.

It was a relief to finally reach him, and to be on the phone rather than the VHF. The radio was handy, but knowing a conversation was being broadcasted changed what got said. Talking candidly about fishing, for example, was not possible.

I asked if the fishing was slow because it was a lull in his day, or if it was slow in a big way.

Just a lull right now, he told me. The fishing had been variable, but was overall better than we'd had that first month.

"Because I'm off the boat?" I blurted.

"No," he laughed. "I'm just finding more fish."

We talked about price. There had been no announcement yet, he said.

I asked, "So you're catching more fish, but not enough to justify a second person?"

That was the case, he said, but the fish size was increasing and the expected bump up in price would probably mean enough income to spell decent wages for me.

I'd cross my fingers and hope, I said, but if nothing

changed in a week, I'd go back to Juneau. I asked him to call by Friday to leave a message on my Juneau phone about whether the fishing was still good.

After that, I parked for a while on the bench in front of the post office, taking in the scenery and enjoying the fact that it wasn't raining. People going by paused to say hi and to give Fidget a friendly pat on the head.

An ATV roared up and halted with a jolt. The owner ran into the post office and a second later reappeared and roared away. His bumper sticker made me laugh. It said: God Is Coming. Look Busy.

Eventually a blond fisherman eased himself down on the edge of the bench I occupied. He held a cardboard box of groceries on his lap, and had a distracted, faraway look on his face. I knew the look. He was likely sleep-deprived, or thinking about fish, or both.

"Hi, Carl."

"Oh, hi, how's it going?" He turned toward me with a courteous bob of his head.

"It's going," I said. "How's the fishing?"

Each fisherman addressed this question differently, based on their particular sense of privacy and the expectations they held for themselves. Plus, variables such as fish availability, size, and price also affected a person's answer. Thus, responses ranged anywhere between a grunt to an hour discourse, depending.

"I'm having some okay days," Carl said and shrugged, "but not enough to make up for the price."

He offered me an apple from his box and took one himself.

We munched companionably while our conversation meandered from fish prices to fish politics to fish recipes. Then the subject swung around to first seasons.

Carl turned out to be a good listener which encouraged me to describe—maybe a bit dramatically—how this, my first season, had hooked me, only to cruelly spit me out on the beach—a failed deckhand.

He grinned at my theatrics and said, "I remember my first season. It ended after only one day."

"Whoa," I said. "What happened?"

He arranged himself more comfortably on the bench, and said, "I came up to work for a longliner."

Longlining was another major fishery associated with Bellport, aside from salmon trolling. Good money could be made going after halibut and black cod on a longline boat, but conditions were often treacherous.

"We weren't even longlining yet. We just went out to catch bait, and we hung the gear up on the bottom."

When gear snags on the bottom, it can do any number of things, and none of them are pleasant. The gear itself can part, which will free the boat, but cost the gear. Otherwise, the gear may hold firm, but then something on the boat must give—typically a more violent event.

Carl continued his story, which involved the more violent scenario. "So we got hung up, and a block broke loose off the mast, hit me in the gut and knocked me overboard."

I stared at him, my eyes wide.

"Yeah," he said. "Mark spun the boat around and got me, luckily, before I sank. Turned out I'd ruptured my pancreas."

I opened and shut my mouth a couple of times like a stunned fish. If he'd gone under in these cold, current-ripped waters, he would not have been found.

"I was sent to Seattle and spent two months there recouping."

"Two months!" I said. "How awful."

Carl looked out over the water. "Well, I thought to myself, okay, injuries occur. This is a setback."

I shook my head, thinking, *I hate setbacks. Setbacks are my mortal enemy*.

"I told my skipper I wanted to come back and fish," he said. "I had it bad."

He had it bad. Something snapped into focus when he said this. All summer I'd been hanging onto the hope that I could get back on the boat. It was just dawning on me that money was not the only reason. I had it bad, too, whatever "it" was.

"Things worked out great," he continued. "Mark was an excellent fisherman; I learned a lot from him. Plus, he's related to John and Betty, and they all became like family to me."

I hadn't known Carl was close to John and Betty. "It's interesting," I said, "how people adopt each other in this place. A lot of us don't have regular families here, so . . ."

"So we find irregular ones," he finished with a grin.

He bid me a friendly good-bye and went on his way, but his story stayed with me. It seemed like there were two ways to look at practically every event that occurred out on this coast. Fishing can rupture your pancreas and make you spend two months in the hospital! But if you persist, you can end up with a great skipper and get to know people like Betty and John. It made me inclined to believe that if you were able to get through the bad parts, the good parts followed.

Nine

THE NEXT DAY MY GOAL was to jig up a halibut, or if that failed, something for lunch at least. The weather was being kind—low clouds, but no rain—so I drifted around in the skiff, reading and occasionally bouncing my bait on the bottom.

It was a pleasure to be lounging in the skiff, getting rocked by the gentle waves in the shadow of some spectacularly beautiful mountains. And to be there holding a book doubled my pleasure. In the past year or two, I'd been so busy with the house remodel I'd I let reading fall by the wayside. It was ironic, because my desire to write came from a love of reading. And my desire to write was what spurred me on to do the house remodel.

Fidget was curled in a ball on the floor of the skiff and a gentle nudge from my foot made her eyes pop open. I showed her my book, a deliciously poignant, funny tome titled *Oldest Living Confederate Widow Tells All*, and said, "Books are important in my life. They nourish me."

She gave me a questioning look. "We lost sight of that, but we're clear about it now, yes?"

She seemed to agree, and I gave her some raisins just for being so cute.

I had a few raisins myself, and realized I should check my line in case I had something, and I did. It was short and fat with bulgy eyes and thick lips. I'd heard the fish called an Irish Lord, and also a Double Ugly, and it did look like a glassy-eyed, overfed rich man with gout and too many chins. I couldn't imagine it tasted very good, so I let it go.

Rebaiting my hook, I bounced it on the bottom and got a little tug right away. I pulled up a black bass. My monster halibut had eluded me for another day, but I had lunch.

The stir-fry I concocted around the bass turned out pretty good, and afterward, some overripe bananas inspired me to make banana bread. I slid the pan of batter into the oven and settled in the chair, unsure whether to read, write a letter to Mary, or scribble ideas for my novel. Despite all the time on my hands I couldn't seem to work up any enthusiasm toward working on my mystery. The books on the cabin shelves just kept calling to me.

Fidget came over to lean against me, and I explained the situation to her. "A big part of being a writer is reading, so I shouldn't feel guilty." She blinked, unsure. "And looking out the window and thinking is also part of being a writer. That takes up a lot of time."

She cocked her head and just looked at me. The truth was, I kept expecting to drop everything and go fishing. That's what I wanted, anyway. I didn't want to write the novel, yet.

My plan, and my nature, dictated that I arrange everything financially so my head would be clear to write.

Fidget waited, hoping I'd say something she could relate to. I remembered the bumper sticker I'd seen on the ATV by the post office and told her: "The Fish Are Coming. Look Busy."

Her brown eyes stayed on me. She seemed convinced that out of my mouth would float particular words she knew, like "go" and "John and Betty" and "skiff".

So I said, "Want to GO in the SKIFF to see JOHN AND BETTY?"

She whirled in circles biting at her tail and went to stand by the door with a wide grin on her chops. Whether she knew it or not, she was making a good point. Books were great, but hanging out with real-life characters was even better.

The timer on the oven dinged, and twenty minutes later I was rapping on John and Betty's door, cradling the warm banana bread in my arms like a swaddled infant. Betty opened the door, saw my cargo, and exclaimed with delight. She set out some butter, John appeared from somewhere, and we cut right into it.

In between bites, I told them I was trying to catch a halibut. I described the spooky creature that bit my hook the other day and John informed me it was probably a skate. Betty jumped up, pulled a book off the shelf and flipped through the pages to show me a picture of one.

"Yep," I said, "it was a skate."

"Let's hope you don't pull up a wolf eel," Betty said,

pointing to another picture. It had vile eyes and a big, down-turned mouth that seemed to be snarling. We shared a mutual shudder.

"Aside from skates and wolf eels," I said, "what other scary things are down there?"

"You might catch a fifty-pound bucket head," John said.

"Lingcod," Betty told me. "He calls them bucket heads because their mouths open so wide."

"Divers will tell you they're aggressive," John said. "They have something like two hundred teeth. Big canines in front."

"They're tasty, though," Betty said.

John nodded. "Good for making fish and chips."

This made me want to catch one and turn it into dinner, while another part of me was thinking: *did he just say two hundred teeth? With big canines in front?*

The subject of fish and chips reminded me to ask whether the Irish Lord was good eating.

"Yes," Betty said, "despite his looks."

We chatted about fish a while longer, and then the subject shifted. John said, "I've been meaning to ask, have you seen any bears out at your place?"

I shook my head no.

"You have an equalizer with you out there?"

An equalizer—in other words, a rifle. "I'm afraid of guns," I confessed.

"You should probably learn to use one."

Dismay washed over me. Tom had always given me the impression that bears rarely came around Steep Cove. It came to mind, though, that on my hike with Flo, she'd whooped to scare off bears, but she'd also carried a rifle.

John noticed my anxious expression, and said, "Well, making noise is a pretty good deterrent." He leaned forward to cut another slab of bread. "Most bears don't want to run into you either."

I'd like to believe that, I thought, *but how do you know?*

He slathered butter all over his bread, nodded at me as though he could read my mind, and said, "A couple of guys I know were out hunting. One of them was walking a ridge and the other was below, walking parallel. They were, oh, maybe a quarter-mile apart."

He paused to take a huge bite. "The guy on top spied this brown bear in the brush, ahead of his partner, right where the man was headed. He got ready to fire his rifle in the air, planning to wave his arms to alert his friend, but then the damned bear slipped behind a tree. It moved right around the tree, staying hidden while the guy went by. It was clear the bear didn't want to be seen. The guy up top watched the whole thing and the guy below never even saw the bear."

This was somewhat reassuring to me, but those guys had guns, too. "What's the word here in town?" I asked. "Have there been any around?"

"Yes!" Betty said. "There's a big one going around and getting into garbage."

A small groan escaped me.

"He left his, well, ah . . ." she paused delicately, " . . . his calling card on the boardwalk the other day. So, everyone is keeping close track of the kids and calling around with reports on where he is."

John was cutting his fourth, or maybe it was his fifth piece of banana bread. Betty casually slid the butter dish out of easy reach, behind a canister of cookies, but with little effort John's long arm found it a half a second later. They both moved without haste, in a contented way that showed just how many years they'd had to work out a system.

"Rachel," Betty continued, "who works at the fish plant, had an encounter with the bear. Ask her and she'll tell you the story."

When she said the word *story*, my pulse quickened. Finding Rachel now topped my to-do list. Entertainment around here is cheap, I thought, but then realized: more than entertainment, I wanted perspective. Just how do people live this close to bears? Was it truly threatening or just inconvenient? How do bears seem to feel about it? How should I feel about it? Tracking down Rachel and hearing her story would shed some light on all this, I figured.

I got up to go, and both John and Betty saw me to the door. Betty gave me one of her warm hugs, and when she released me, impulsively I turned and gave John a quick hug. Caught off guard, he froze, and it made me smile. This big, strapping Norwegian man was hard to ruffle—unless you surprised him with a hug.

~~~~~

Rachel, the woman with the bear story, was someone I'd seen outside the fish processing plant during afternoon break, taking a cigarette. Break was in an hour so I had time for a milk shake.
~~~~~

At the cafe, I slid onto a stool at the counter and greeted Kay. She and her husband, Nicko, ran the place.

"What's new?" she asked, handing me the milk shake.

"I caught a skate," I announced.

A guy at a nearby table said, "A skate? They're good fertilizer."

"They are?"

"Sure," he said. "We caught one, oh, about eight feet long and buried it in an old skiff we were using for a garden container." He beamed. "You should see the wild strawberries hanging out of that skiff now."

"Good eating, too," chimed in a young fisherman I'd seen around. "Skate wings. You cut them in strips, sauté them up. They have a texture a lot like scallops."

It flitted across my mind that they might be pulling my leg, which happened sometimes to newcomers, but there were no winks or snickers. *They're not teasing me,* I thought with a rush of pleasure, *they're* including *me.*

A woman appeared at my elbow. "I heard you slapped Louie," she said, taking the spot at the counter next to me.

I'd seen her around but couldn't recall her name. "No," I said slowly, "I'm pretty sure I never slapped Louie." A guy in his late sixties, Louie was fond of grabbing women. But he liked women with big busts.

Kay piped up. "That was the other Carol, who used to work in the store. She slapped him, and it was a good slap." That Carol had an abundant figure, and abundant attitude to go with it. Everyone laughed, picturing Louie getting his due.

The door swung wide and a tourist came in. Studying the menu written on the dry-erase board, he asked Nicko, "What are you known for?"

We all thought he'd say the borscht, but Nicko threw a look at Kay and said, "Closing early."

Kay leaned close and whispered to me, "We cut out early yesterday afternoon." Her tone was conspiratorial, and her eyes were shining, so of course my mind jumped to hanky panky. *Wow, that's kind of a lot of information* I thought, until she added, still speaking in an undertone that pulsed with happiness, "We went king fishing. I guess this means we're going again today."

I should have known the subject was . . . fishing!

Kay asked if I was going to do any more trolling with Tom this season.

I told her hopefully, but so far he hadn't needed me. "In the meantime I'm eager for work if you hear of anything."

"Something will come along," she said with sweet conviction. "I'll pass the word."

Right then we both noticed the cafe door wasn't closed all the way, and there was Fidget's face, peering in at me. Her expression said: *Can I come in, please? I'm worried you might trip over those crumbs I see on the floor. I feel it is my duty to clean them up, for your safety.*

"Hey, I have something for her!" Kay went in the back and reappeared with a bag of snacks.

I thanked her and headed back down the boardwalk. Reaching the fish plant, I loitered outside, waiting to ask Rachel about her story.

TEN

THE BREAK BELL RANG and Rachel, a lean woman in her forties, stepped out of the plant to light her cigarette. We nodded hello and commented on the day's mild weather and then I confessed my mission was to hear her story about the big bear hanging around town.

She said, "Yeah, I almost ran into that bear on my bicycle."

"No!"

"I'm serious. I was riding my bike to work, about six in the morning, and he was out of sight by the dumpster. I rode by, and here's this big bear just a few feet away. A minute later somebody on foot spooked him and he started running, going in the same direction as me. I looked back and he was coming up right behind me."

"Oh my God."

"Yeah, I started pedaling for my life. I could hear him snorting. Then my chain came off, and I wiped out. I just curled up in a ball and covered my head and thought, okay, this is it."

She paused to take a hit on her cigarette. I felt like shouting SO WHAT HAPPENED THEN?

After exhaling, she went on, "I couldn't hear him anymore but was afraid to look, afraid he'd be right there. But then the suspense got to me. I peeked, and he was gone. He musta cut through the patio between those two buildings," she pointed with her cigarette, "and jumped off the boardwalk. I went into work but couldn't stop thinking about it. Three, four hours later I was still a wreck, so my boss finally told me to go home for the rest of the day."

Not a lot of people go home early from work for that reason, I thought.

The bell rang to end the break. She stubbed out her cigarette, nodded to me and headed back into the clanging, echoing mouth of the fish plant.

Back at Steep Cove, after I landed the skiff, my eyes probed the deep green woods lining the thin strip of rocky beach. It wasn't hard to imagine a bear barreling out and chewing me up. It made me feel light in the chest and all tingly up the back of my scalp. *Primal fear,* I told myself, *pay attention to how it feels. You can use it in your fiction.*

A branch snapped in the woods and I stared, bug-eyed, in that direction. Holding my breath, I strained to hear. My ears grew larger and angled forward like a dog's. Okay, that last bit didn't actually happen, but that's how my ears *felt.*

One hundred yards separated me from the cabin. I started out walking, but my legs began moving faster and faster while my brain shouted: *Don't run! Everyone says don't run!* I ended up in a full sprint, my adrenal glands shouting, *Run! You're prey!*

Ushering Fidget inside, I slammed the door closed so hard it shook the flimsy cabin. I had no interest in any further study of primal fear, I decided. That Pulitzer Prize just wasn't worth it.

For the next hour, I sat in the chair eating handfuls of Cheerios out of the box and thinking, of course, about bears. It worried me that someone as experienced and wise as John would tell me to get a gun for protection.

Other than hunting earlier in the summer with Dennis, my only other close encounter with a gun happened in Crete. A Greek man, Michalis, took me on a date. We gathered sea salt from the rocks that lined the island's shore; he was going to sell it for cash. I fell in love right there—guys who make a living from the sea, my weakness, grrrr. Afterward, he made me dinner at his bungalow—a man who cooks, double grrrr.

After dinner, he took my hand and led me out into the backyard where he shot his pistol at the black night sky. Argh! Love affair over.

Fidget came over to rest her head on my knee, tugging me back to the present. I rubbed her ears and let out a big sigh. One good thing about being in a cabin with only a dog for company—heavy sighing was allowed.

Looking out the window, I realized that the beach in front of the cabin was a metaphor for my present situation. It was littered with logs, which Tom had captured from around the inlet, towed home, and tied off near the cabin.

He planned to cut them up for firewood. Twice a day the tide came up and went back out, and it moved these logs around on their tethers. To get to the skiff, the first part of the walk involved negotiating a cat's cradle of lines and logs criss-crossing everywhere. Every time I walked to get to the skiff, nothing was the same, because the tide was perpetually shifting the logs around.

And, just like those logs, my circumstances kept shifting. I struggled sometimes to keep my footing, because nothing stayed constant.

I started out as a deckhand, then a boat painter and a cook, followed by Huck Finn subsistence girl. And now, I'm supposed to learn to shoot a gun to defend myself against bears? *I did* not *sign myself up for all these classes! There's been a mistake. I demand to see a school counselor.*

I hated being so unsettled by the challenges of this life, and fearful, but that's how I felt. And my fearfulness about bears wasn't even based on an actual bear encounter. I was sitting here stuffing Cheerios in my mouth, freaked out by the mere idea of them. Meanwhile, the local folks went around acting nonplussed about the real thing—a big one on the boardwalk: oh, jeepers, better keep track of the kids!

These islanders had a certain equanimity that set them apart, a quality I thought of as "Alaska-ness." There was Flo shrugging over the forgotten broccoli, and substituting a beach green, and Betty climbing out a boat window to give that eagle's beak "some room." And John, so high up on that ladder, patiently swinging that heavy hammer to pry off the ironbark. He was, what, in his seventies?

Even serious problems, ones with disaster potential, were faced with admirable calm. I thought about Carl, calling his busted pancreas a "setback." And that pilot in the wheeled plane—his life was in danger until some level-headed stranger came up with the idea that he follow the faint white curl of the surf in the dark.

My neighbors would scoff if I suggested it to them, but braving the things this island life threw at a human, it required courage. Or, at the very least, it required not running away when a problem loomed.

I had to laugh then, thinking about how I'd just run down the beach to get away from the bear that wasn't even real.

So then I started thinking about how, in addition to a challenging environment, people also helped shape people. My neighbors had already taught me a lot, it made me wonder if, just by hanging around with them, I might absorb some of their "Alaska-ness."

It was a silly idea, perhaps, but one thing I knew for sure: cowering in the cabin wasn't the path to absorbing anything, except maybe Cheerios.

I launched out of the chair and stood before the VHF. Ginger, one of my Steep Cove neighbors, was someone I didn't know very well, but I wanted to. She was ten years older than me, a statuesque, outgoing woman with an enviable mane of wavy brown hair. Her husband went out trolling with one of their grown sons while she remained on the beach, cultivating a lush vegetable garden and making gorgeous pottery.

I picked up the radio mic, thinking I'd ask her to dinner

and ply her with questions about her experiences. People socialized with ease in these parts, so calling a neighbor up like this was fine. But even so, I hesitated. She was someone I admired. What if she didn't like me?

When she came back to my radio call, I cleared my throat and asked if she'd like to come over for dinner.

"I'll bring a pie," she said instantly. "What time?"

A while later, when she pulled up in her skiff, I went out to help with the outhaul. On the way back to the cabin, she lost her footing on one of the kelp-covered treasures Tom had lying around the beach; I think it was once a door. She was fine but the pie fell, and the glass dish cracked right down the middle.

We got inside and examined the damage, and saw we could still eat the pie if we stayed away from the break.

We were both hungry so right away we ladled up bowls of seafood chowder. She claimed the beanbag chair and I took the armchair, and after a few spoonfuls of soup, she looked at me kindly and asked, "So how are things going?"

"I have no clue what I'm doing."

She wriggled, settling herself better in the beanbag chair, and said, "Yeah, when I got here, I didn't know anything."

I put my spoon down in surprise. The woman sprawled in front of me like some kind of beanbag queen was truly one of the most confident women I'd ever met. It was hard to believe that she'd ever felt unsure.

"It's intimidating when you're new, but you're not as alone as it seems." Remembering, she said, "My youngest son was born at the cabin. I was still so new around here, few people even knew I was pregnant. Right after he was born, I skiffed into Bellport to weigh him on the post office scale. Betty came up to me and gave me a present—gift-wrapped and everything! She had seen me skiff by her house and came to find me at the post office, to show me that kindness. I didn't even think she knew I was pregnant!"

I observed that it must have been rough, giving birth in a Steep Cove cabin.

She grinned. "I was in labor for an hour and forty-nine minutes—is that cool or what?"

Laughing, I said, "You're blowing my mind, you know."

"With kids, you just do what you do," she shrugged. "Then, the next thing you know, they're grown up. It's really nice when they're grown up."

I took a breath. "Yeah," I said, "they grow into their own people."

"And their own shoes," she said. "The happiest day of my life was when both my sons finally grew out of my boot size. Graduation was cool, the birth of two grandkids—those milestones were great, but that day when they finally left my rubber boots alone . . ." she shook her head, "that was truly grand."

I burst out laughing. What a roller-coaster ride of a talk this was, and we were just getting started.

I asked her to describe what life was like in Bellport, back when she first arrived.

Ginger thought for a moment. "We had this community hall, and it was the absolute heart of the community. It was this rickety old Quonset hut with a sticker on the door:

enter at your own risk. We held dances there, played bingo. We'd pile in to watch *African Queen* or *The Sound of Music*, and everyone would bring pillows, 'cause they only had those hard folding chairs, and we'd eat bags of homemade popcorn."

She paused to take in a spoonful of chowder. "You always wanted to get there an hour early for a good seat because the whole town would turn out."

She clattered her spoon down into her bowl. "How 'bout some of that pie?"

Her rhubarb custard pie was delicious—tart and creamy. As we savored dessert, she continued. "But you know what? When satellite TV came, everything changed. At first, the only TV we had here was homegrown, and that was great, actually. This guy had a beta player, and a cable strung from his living room, out along the boardwalk, in and out of houses. Someone recorded TV programs down in the Lower 48, and mailed him the tapes. When the plane didn't make it in, he would put on old tapes, reruns, sometimes for weeks, but people still watched. When he forgot to change the tape or if he fell asleep, people'd call him up and say, 'Hey, put another tape in.'

"But then this woman decided to bring satellite T.V. into Bellport, claiming it would keep people out of the bars. She got a grant, and right after the town got satellite T.V., Perseverance Theatre came over from Juneau to perform a play, and the Quonset hut was half-empty. I asked people why they missed the play, and they said, 'Well, Dallas was on.'" She gave a snort. "And now, of course, the bar has satellite T.V., with countless channels, duh."

Neither of us said anything then; we just looked out the window. I thought about how some currents in our culture seem to be moving us farther away from one another, but there were also many forces that drew us together. The ones that brought people together, to my mind, were the more powerful and enduring.

I was thinking, of course, about pie.

"So what do you think?" I asked my guest. "Should we go for seconds on dessert?"

"I'm game," she said, and we dished up two more pieces, leaving a thin strip of pie over the break in the plate.

After we settled back in our seats, I told Ginger I had more questions about life at Steep Cove and she said, "Sure."

Thinking of bears, I asked, "Weren't you scared for your kids?"

"Yeah," she said. "Earthquakes, for example, will get you thinking."

"Earthquakes?" I gulped. That hadn't even occurred to me.

Ginger said, "Once, about four in the morning, we had a good trembler. It woke all of us up. The guys just turned over and went back to sleep but I was too awake. I went outside and couldn't believe my eyes. There were live clams all over the beach, lying on top of the sand. They must have been shook to the surface by the quake. So I got a five-gallon bucket and before anyone else was up, I had it overflowing with clams."

Her tale about this odd windfall made me smile, until she added, "I had trouble sleeping because, of course, after a big earthquake, there's always the worry about tsunamis."

"Tsunamis?" I asked weakly.

"Yeah. There was one tsunami years ago, but since then we've only had warnings. NOAA has issued lots of warnings over the years, come to think of it."

"If there's a warning . . . what do we do?"

"It depends. Some people charge out to the middle of the inlet and wait in their boats, hoping they can ride it out. People onshore, they try to get some elevation. I remember one time I was home alone with the boys and a trembler came. Right afterward we got a tsunami warning—word went out over the VHF. The boys and I ran around throwing food and clothing in five-gallon buckets and then we climbed up into the woods behind the house.

"We sat there a couple of hours. These were teenage boys, you know, so of course they ate all our food up in the first hour. I had no way of knowing if it was all clear—we had no handheld radios back then—so I made the boys stay and climbed down to use the house VHF, figuring if the warning was still on, I'd run back up the hill. It was a creepy feeling, wondering if that wave could be seconds away. Finally someone came back to my call and told me it was over."

She raised her hand to point outside. Framed by the cabin window, a blue heron poised on one leg at the inlet's edge, silhouetted against the indigo sky. "God, that's a painting," she murmured.

We sat, just looking at the gorgeous view. Then quietly,

she said, “You know, when a place happens to you . . .” her voice trailed off.

Like that heron outside, I held myself still and hopeful, waiting for her to finish the sentence. But instead she gave a big yawn, and said it was probably time for her to head home.

After she pulled away, her hair tossing wildly behind her, I stood on the beach for a while, smelling the salty air, and the question rang in my head: What *does* happen when a place happens to you?

ELEVEN

I WENT JIGGING AT DAWN and stayed at it all day, despite frequent rain showers. *You have to put in your hours.* That's what people said about trying to jig up a halibut. Another handy phrase I repeated to myself that day was: *nothing worthwhile happens fast.*

Finally, something took my bait. It wasn't a halibut, but a lingcod. John had indicated that they could reach fifty pounds or more, but this one was only about seven pounds. That was fine with me, considering all those teeth. They were installed in a mouth that opened eerily wide, making it clear why John had nicknamed them bucket heads.

With dinner in the skiff, my stomach started grumbling so I quit around six o'clock. The lingcod fillets, cooked simply with butter, salt, and pepper, made a gorgeous meal. I washed my plate and considered what to do with my evening. One possibility was to attend an event in town, something called a ham bowl. The purpose of it was to raise funds for next summer's Fourth of July fireworks.

I figured it was probably some sort of dish being auctioned off, which didn't sound especially exciting to me, but I felt it was my civic duty to at least show up.

I should have guessed that doing one's civic duty in Bellport was not at all boring, and even had a bit of twisted fun built into it.

Dear Mary,

You asked in your last letter what I've been up to. I'll fill you in, but first I'd like to sympathize with you about your hubby: I agree! Why can't he take out the trash *and* put a new liner in the can, like you keep asking. Finish the job, guy!

Now, as for what I've been up to: Last night there was a gathering at the bar. While I was there, three people hit the floor and I talked to two guys with their flies down.

I get the impression this wasn't an unusual night, as far as those things go. The atypical part of the evening was the fund-raiser, something called a ham bowl, which, I discovered, was an evening of bowling.

The prize was a ham and because we eat so much fish around here, people wanted that ham, and they wanted it bad.

Bellport lacks a bowling alley, so the "lane" was the floor of the bar, between the pool table and the bathroom. Plastic pop bottles filled with sand worked for pins, and the bowling ball was—get this—a Cornish hen. It started out frozen and slid like crazy at first, but got more sluggish as the evening wore on. (People adjusted their game accordingly.) The jubilant winner took home the ham, and the person with the lowest score got the Cornish hen.

It was an interesting night, conversation-wise,

in between turns. Somehow we got on the subject of teeth, and Peggy (the cafe has one waitress, and she's the one) leaned toward me and said, "After I take my turn, I'll tell you about getting my sore tooth pulled." She tapped her finger on the counter. "I was sitting right here, at the bar."

When she got back from her turn with the Cornish hen, she said, "I had a couple of loose teeth, but this one molar was really bothering me. I didn't have a lot of money at the time, so I couldn't afford the $250 plane fare into Juneau and back, plus hotel, plus the dentist." She continued after ordering another beer. "I was in here on a slow night, just me and two guys in the whole bar. I said something about my molar and one of them offered to pull it for me. I asked him, 'Got a string?'"

I shook my head in wonder, thinking that was the end of the story, but she said, "Unfortunately, he pulled the wrong one." She laughed at my you-gotta-be-kidding look. "So after a couple more shots of whiskey, we tied the string again, and that time we pulled the right one."

So then Mara, who was sitting with us, offered up her tooth story. "When I was a kid, we got twenty-five cents per tooth from the tooth fairy. At least that's what I *thought*. So one day I looked in the mirror and saw all those teeth and thought, hey, I know a way I can make a buck or two. So I bought one of those Sugar Daddies, remember those? Toffee on a stick? I bit down on that thing for a while, really dug my teeth in. When I yanked it out, I had five of my baby teeth in that sucker. I put them under my pillow and guess what? In the morning, all I got was twenty-five cents. I cried and cried."

We were all laughing.

"Not because of my teeth," she paused, "but because that fairy was one cheap *son of a bitch*!"

She took a swig of her beer, and I felt like cheering, her delivery was so good.

So to answer your question, sis, ham bowling is what I've been up to.

And just for the record, none of those people who hit the floor last night was me. And those boys I saw with their zippers down? They weren't trying to scare anybody, they just forgot to finish one thing before starting another . . . kinda like your hubby forgetting the trash can liner.

Okay, well . . . stay tuned.

xxoo

Carole

~~~~~

The next couple of days it poured outside, and I spent long hours reading. On the third morning I opened my eyes and my first thought was that fairies had snuck around in the middle of the night, wrapping the cabin in gauze.

Staring at the blank fog outside the window, it dawned on me that it was Friday, my cutoff date for returning to Juneau. Unless Tom had left a message saying fishing had improved, it was time to get myself packed.

Fifty-some straight hours of rain didn't bum me out, nor did the dense fog now pressing against the window. But the idea that I might be switching this world out for Juneau suddenly made me cranky.

I needed to go into town and check my messages, but the woodstove was giving off such a cozy, fragrant heat, and I was deep into a good book. It was hard to switch gears.
~~~~~

It was the quest for food, barbecued food in particular, that finally spurred me to action. I'd heard talk on the VHF concerning a party—everyone was invited—on the flats that afternoon.

The first thing I did upon reaching the boardwalk was go to the payphone and try Tom's number. He was out of range but had left a message the day before. The fishing had turned a corner. It was hot, he said. He planned to sell his fish Friday evening at the scow and would call me on the radio afterward so we could plan our rendezvous.

I closed my eyes and leaned my head against the cold glass of the payphone booth. For whatever reason, Tom was finally catching a good load of fish. Gratitude and relief coursed through me. "Sounds like a backhoe situation to me!" was my message back to him. "I'll talk to you tonight."

A month of the season remained. It was enough time, I thought. We could still hit the mother lode. With all the faith I'd shown, a fairy-tale ending to this summer just seemed like the only kind of ending possible.

Hungry and excited to see people, I hustled down the boardwalk with Fidget trotting at my side. Down where the boards ended and the flats began, the barbecue party was in full swing.

The tide was out. I pointed to the gloriously open space fanning out before us and explained to Fidget that this was flat land, and it was okay to go play on it.

She took my suggestion to mean, *go stand by the nearest soft-hearted person holding a paper plate and stare at them with big eyes.* I had to laugh because she scored a morsel before I even had my paper plate in hand.

The grill was fixed in place at the edge of the flats, an industrial-sized monster that was perpetually rusted because the surf got to it on stormy high tides. People just scraped the worst rust off with a wire brush, and it was good to go.

Huge slabs of halibut and salmon sizzled over the coals seductively, but I had no interest in the fish once my eyes landed on the platter of venison steaks, grilled and ready for takers.

I was about halfway through my second plate of food—this time I conceded to take a few chicken legs—when the boiling purple clouds overhead parted and rain started dumping on our heads.

With no cover nearby, we stood around, trying to keep our food from getting soggy in the deluge. Lightning crackled and because on this coast lightning was rare, people got excited. They took deep sniffs of the charged air and said it reminded them of other places they'd lived.

A fisherman walked up to the cooler, got a beer, and said quietly that he had some news from the buyers on the price—some bad news. He soberly explained that the price on salmon had dropped, and it was rumored another drop would come soon.

A ripple of shock ran through the crowd, and then everyone started talking at once. Some people said that this was just an aberration, and the price was bound to stabilize and rise. Others expressed anger that farmed fish could impact the wild fish market so drastically, because the two products weren't even in the same class.

I threw away my plate, called for Fidget and rushed down the boardwalk to the payphone. Tom was waiting in line to sell at the scow and picked up on the first ring. The price had dropped, he confirmed.

In simple terms it meant he'd make about fifteen percent less on this current load of fish than anticipated. Fifteen percent is a deckhand's cut, I thought.

I told him rumors were circulating that the price could keep spiraling downward. He stayed silent, and that made me ache, because when he couldn't be cheerful, Tom got quiet.

"Does this put the botch on me joining you out there?" I asked.

"I think so," was his sober reply.

He told me to leave Fidget with John and Betty when I left for Juneau; they'd watch her until he could come pick her up.

Leave Fidget? My throat tightened.

He said his turn to sell had come up and he had to say goodbye. I hung up and struggled to get my disappointment under control. I had calls to make. I had to arrange a place to stay in Juneau, plus I needed to rustle up work.

Fidget was waiting for me outside the phone booth. She was soaking wet, muddy from the flats, and standing very still, her shining eyes fixed anxiously on my face.

Those calls were necessary, but I didn't have the heart to make them yet. Not knowing what else to do, I returned to the barbecue.

Walking back toward the flats I had many things to consider, but all I could think was how much I'd miss Fidget. Until then, I hadn't really appreciated how constant she was in her affections, and how her company sweetened my days.

My heart was in my boots. Why did the stupid buyers have to lower the price?

Reaching the flats, I dug a beer out of one of the ice chests and stood by a clump of people hanging around the grill. A woman about my age, Laura, looked over and smiled.

I took a step closer and blurted, "Can I ask you a question?"

"Okay . . ." She looked wary, and even took a little step away.

I unclenched my fists, and reminded myself that most people did not instantly launch into their deepest, most anxious thoughts; typically people eased into conversation.

"I was wondering . . . wondering, ah . . ." I pointed. "Do you know what kind of duck that is?" As soon as the words flew from my mouth, I could see it was a mallard. So now she was going to think I was socially inept, *plus* stupid.

"That's a mallard," Laura said, and added kindly, "I think."

"Oh, yeah," I said. Giving up on conversational openers, I let fly. "So what I'm really wondering is this: Why do people even live here? There's fresh fish to eat and it's beautiful, but mostly what's here is a *lack* of things—things like economic security. And if there's an abundance of anything, it's hazards! And uncertainty! Why do people put up with the hassles!"

My rant stopped abruptly, and I wondered if Laura

would opt to put a little more distance between us, like maybe a few hundred yards, but she just said thoughtfully, "Well, I don't know why people live here. It's a good question."

We gazed around and I assumed we were finished with the topic, but then she continued. "My mom always asked me the same thing. 'Why are you living there?' she would ask. 'It's a town of misfits.' And I always just told her, 'Mom, I guess it's because I don't want to fit in anywhere else.'"

She laughed, took a bite of potato salad, and said, "I remember when we first moved here, my sister and I thought it was the end of the world. We were just kids and when we learned there was no TV, we burst into tears. I can remember counting every crack in the boardwalk, we were so bored." She stepped over and got more fish from the grill before continuing. "But then, three years later, when my parents said we were moving back south, we cried again, because we hated to leave our friends." She ate a forkful of black cod. "I vowed to come back and I did. The summer I was nineteen I came to work at the fish plant." She gave a rueful laugh. "I was going to leave in August, but never did."

"Why did you stay?"

She shrugged. "There was always plenty of work."

I looked at her doubtfully. "Like at the fish plant?"

"That, and other things. I owned a pizza place."

"Really?"

"Yeah, we just called it The Pizza Place. And for a while I did laundry. I charged per pound—weighed before it got washed. Sometimes out of curiosity I weighed it afterward and would see a three- to five-pound difference! Not something you wanna think too much about, actually."

We raised our beers to that. "Later I started working for the floatplane company. It was just supposed to be one day a week, but it turned into every day, which was a bit wearing." She shook her head. "Dealing with people, especially people who aren't from here, can be funny, or annoying, depending. One time I had some big people scheduled to fly. By 'big' I don't mean important—I mean *huge people*. So these planes have a certain weight limit—pilot's weight, plus fuel, plus passengers. And the weight of these passengers, without any baggage, put the plane over limit. They insisted they all had to get on that plane. I told them, okay, but you can't take any baggage. We'll send it on the next plane. They started arguing with me. They kept saying, 'We're *allowed* fifty pounds of luggage.' I almost said to them, 'People, you are *wearing* your fifty pounds.'" She gave a short laugh. "Needless to say, we sent their baggage on the next plane."

We chatted a while longer, and eventually I told her about my disappointment over how the summer had failed to produce any income.

"Bummer," she nodded sympathetically. "But you know that saying about how money doesn't make you rich? I've been thinking about that lately. I guess because the other day I made my daughter a scrapbook and it made me realize no matter how much money you have, what really makes you rich are your memories."

Very true, I responded, but silently I was thinking about another truth alongside that one. She had a daughter, and a rich store of memories built around that legacy. The legacy I wanted for myself was to become an author. So I needed to get back to Juneau, where I had the means to do that.

Twelve

Back at the cabin, I stuffed things into a duffel bag and tried to ignore an inner voice that kept insisting I didn't have to leave. That I could stick around a bit longer. That I could keep finding odd jobs to make ends meet.

But just making ends meet was not enough, I told myself sternly. It was fine when I was younger, when I was footloose and lacking specific goals, but those days were over. It was time for me to grow up.

My bothersome inner voice demanded: Does growing up have to be the opposite of *growing*?

The price was going *down*, I reminded myself. Everything was just going to get tighter, and to consider staying went against reason. The economy on this island was a crazy tightrope walk, with no safety net. Case closed.

The following day I went to arrange my flight out, but paused on the boardwalk, mentally saying good-bye to the view. It took me a while to notice someone was leaning against the railing next to me, giving me a sideways look.

It was Bernice, a long-term resident of Bellport. Over

eighty and no taller than my rib cage, she was known and loved by everyone in town, but especially by the males. A masterful flirt, she had every guy in town crazy about her.

She greeted me by asking in her movie star's loaded-with-promise voice, "How's Tom?"

"Leave my man alone," I growled.

She laughed and we stood for a moment, taking in the view. Then she said, "I was in the cafe and Kay mentioned you're looking for work. You want to help me with some housecleaning?"

Even though she sure didn't act like it, Bernice was the oldest person in town, and if you counted experience I'd be voted the youngest. For the privilege of her company, I would have done anything for her, for free.

But the look she was giving me was unmistakable. It said: *When you're flush, you can do something for me and refuse to take money. But that's not now, missy.*

It made me both nervous and elated to realize my strict view of economy hadn't taken into account at least one important variable. The economy in this place was a crazy tightrope walk, that much was true. But I was beginning to see that there was a safety net. *People* were the safety net.

Could I let this little bit of insurance overturn my intention to leave? Could I not run?

My wish was to stay longer. I wanted to hang out with Bernice, and Flo, and John and Betty, and hear more stories, and learn everything I could from them.

It wasn't my original goal for the summer, but in just a few short weeks something in me had shifted. Maybe a little Alaska-ness was rubbing off on me.

I told Bernice, "I can start now, if you want."

She laughed at my eagerness. "Come by tomorrow," she said. "I'll have cookies."

Back at the payphone, I left a message for Tom that my plan was to stick around for a while longer.

I stopped in the store to stock up on some groceries, and after stashing them in the skiff, went down to the bar. A loaf of bread rode in my backpack, an extra to give away. I had in mind this one man; he always looked sad, and was always there on the same bar stool.

Since we were strangers and he was, of course, drunk, my intention started to slip upon seeing him. But, blushing, I went ahead and asked if he wanted this loaf of bread I happened to have in my backpack.

He gave the golden, pudgy loaf a look of wonder, and then reached out and drew it to his chest like it was a long-wished-for puppy. He asked if I played cribbage and I told him no, and he said he'd teach me anytime I wanted.

The bar owner saw the bread and offered to buy some the next time I made a batch. So suddenly, in addition to Bernice's work offer, I had a way to break even on my beer drinking.

I walked out of the bar puffed up with goodwill, convinced that fortune would continue to kiss my deserving brow. I was, in other words, begging the universe to have a little fun with me, and right away it did.

First, I got back to my skiff to find my groceries had been raided, and my eggs were gone.

The egg container was on the floor of the skiff, open, a bit tattered, with just a few tiny traces of eggshell and egg. I had covered my groceries with a raincoat, knowing about the canny ravens, but today that precaution failed. The birds had pulled back the raincoat, rummaged through my purchases, passed over the cookies, celery, and canned goods, opened the cardboard egg container, and had somehow airlifted away, or devoured on the spot, my dozen eggs.

The store had closed by this time, so I skiffed toward home, annoyed to have been outwitted by birdbrains. But halfway there, my mood flipped around because I found a good firewood log, floating unclaimed. I attached a towline and merrily brought it home, hauled out the skiff, and went up to the cabin.

Dear Mary,

I'm at the cabin, parked in the armchair next to the window, eating dinner. Have I mentioned that the cabin lacks a table? You hardly miss it, because the chair has these wide, flat arms—the perfect resting place for your coffee cup, sandwich plate, or your elbows while you hold a book. The chair also has a couple of other wonderful features. It's angled just right for taking in the view, and has deep cushions that invite sitting for hours.

I paused. In this letter, I wanted to work my way around to bragging to Mary about finding that firewood log. It was a sweet find, and I was elated about it, but for her to understand I'd have to explain some things.

If you burned a woodstove for heat, then your supply of firewood was always in the back of your mind. This log would provide not only wood, but good-burning wood. It was thoroughly dead, not the slightest bit green, and it had been floating high so I knew it was wet on the outside but not waterlogged. Its branches were long gone, scoured off against rough beaches, so it just needed to be cut in rounds, and then split and stacked.

Aglow with smug satisfaction, I swept the beach with my gaze, looking for my prize.

I couldn't see it anywhere, and it took me a minute to understand why. After tugging it safely home, I'd forgotten to tie the towline to anything. So the high tide had come and gently floated it away.

The universe wasn't done laughing yet. A short while later, I started thinking about a bath and went to fill the tub. That's when I found out: the cabin water had quit.

This wasn't a problem, I told myself, but an adventure. I grabbed Tom's bucket of plumbing parts and climbed up the creek. Two falls and a banged knee later, I reached the intake pipe, and saw the problem. A tree had torn loose from the bank upstream and had come tumbling down to dislodge the pipe.

Fixing it required dissembling a section of waterline and replacing a small length of crushed pipe. I had to deal with a bunch of hose clamps, and being screwdriver handicapped, kept forgetting which way tightened and which way loosened the clamps. But then I remembered the saying *right-tighty-lefty-loosey*, and it worked. I'd probably still be up that creek, cursing like crazy, if it wasn't for that rhyme.

After relocating the intake pipe, I climbed back down the slippery creek, opened a valve, and got nothing but tooting sounds. I scrambled back up and poured a bunch of water in the pipe. I went back down and still only got a trickle. I went back up and poured more water in the pipe, went back down, eased the valve open, and got tooting sounds *and* a trickle.

This kind of seat-of-the-rain-pants-plumbing went on for a few hours. The whole time I just kept doing things that I'd seen Tom do, without really understanding the point of any of it. Finally, when that steady gush of water came through the pipes and into the sink, it first seemed like a miracle. But I quickly embraced it as an accomplishment, even though I wasn't sure how I did it.

I turned the kitchen faucet on and off to admire my work, put my arms up like Rocky, and danced around the cabin shouting to no one, *I fixed it!* Suddenly I glimpsed myself in the mirror—baggy clothing, matted-down hair, muddy chin—and went dashing for the bath.

I embarked upon history's longest, steamiest, and proudest bath ever, reveling in the knowledge that *I* personally got that water to come down the creek and into the tub.

I indulged in the regular girly rituals—scented candles, bath oil, hair pampering, wishing my legs were less football player and more Marilyn Monroe, telling myself that it didn't matter because I had a good heart, then telling myself *that* didn't matter, because good wasn't the same as shapely.

Screw shapely, I concluded, and built a bubble unicorn horn on my forehead.

~~~~~

The next day brought pounding rain. I geared up in full-body rubber, crossed my fingers that the water pipe would stay secure in the thundering creek, and went to clean house for Bernice.

While working I pestered her with questions, asking, for starters, what she liked about Bellport.

She told me she liked everything about it, except for one thing. "I hate to fly," she said. "Those damn floatplanes rattle so much it's like you can hear the screws working loose." She flicked her cigarette, disgusted. "The last time I went to Juneau, on the way back I asked the pilot, 'How much longer to Bellport?' He said five minutes, and I said, 'Well, buddy, you'd better make it a *fast* five minutes. I'll be damned if I'm going to vomit in my new purse.'"

The whole day went like this, me asking questions, and Bernice telling stories that made me laugh.

She originally came to Bellport to help a friend move here, but stayed because the fish plant needed workers. "There was so much work, we were doing massive overtime. You needed a sense of humor just to stay sane." By now we were taking a coffee break at her kitchen table. She waggled a finger at my empty cup, and I obediently poured myself another as she continued, "It always helped when we got a batch of fresh workers, because we liked to play jokes on the new people. Like with the cold shots."
~~~~~

"The what?" I asked.

"You know we worked in freezers that were minus forty or fifty degrees, right?" I nodded. "So each season we convinced the new batch of plant workers that they needed inoculation shots against the cold."

"No way."

"Way . . ." She drew the word out like a teenager and grinned. "The town had a butcher back then, and this guy happened to mount crabs—like a taxidermist. He had this huge, long needle for injecting the crab with whatever he injected them with, so when the new workers came each spring, we'd line them up outside the office and this guy would wear his butcher's smock and hold up that big needle and take the first person by the arm and bring them in the office. He'd tell them the joke and instruct them to start screaming like hell. Some people waiting in line actually ran to get a seat on the next plane out of town. It kinda weeded out the wimps." She pulled on her cigarette and exhaled with a long, satisfied sigh.

After talking our way through several plates of cookies and cups of coffee, it was time to leave. Bernice stepped out onto the boardwalk with me. The rain had let up and we stood by her door, idly admiring the hummingbirds. Six of them darted around our heads, filling the air with indignant clicks, their beaks sticking out like sewing needles.

"Find a quiet spot and hold your hand out," Bernice said, "and a hummingbird will land on your palm."

I was about to try, but just then a golf cart zoomed up and we were joined by Mara, coming by to ask Bernice a question about the Elvis quilt that they were working on.

I'd heard these two ladies were best friends and it had surprised me, considering Mara was in her fifties and Bernice was eighty-something. But seeing them together, I believed it. They instantly began joshing one another, and underneath the teasing was a special ease, a certain deep familiarity you get only with someone you know well and hold dear. It caused a start of recognition in me.

In the past, I'd had this kind of unique click with a friend in college, and again a few years later in Chicago with my housemate of four years. Though my current circle of friends in Juneau was wonderfully wide, I couldn't think of any one person with whom I was truly close. One reason was probably Tom—we got involved right after I moved to Juneau and that became my primary relationship. But the house project was probably the main reason. My friendships weren't as deep these last few years, because the remodel gobbled up time.

So that made two things I'd bartered away by focusing so hard on the house remodel: I'd stopped reading, and had paid less attention to friendships. Fixing up the house was a solid goal, and I was willing to make sacrifices, but it made sense to recognize what those sacrifices were and what they cost.

Watching the two women exchange banter, their faces relaxed and beaming, I hoped I could keep this lesson in mind: we don't need a ton of friends in our lives, and we don't need friends in our same generation. We just need people with whom we can truly relate.

Eventually, I said good-bye and eased on down the boardwalk, but turned for a last look. The two women stood together, laughing heartily, surrounded by glinting, feasting hummingbirds. It looked like a Disney moment until Bernice raised a hand and batted a hummingbird away, just like one would swat at a mosquito.

~~~~~

Later that week another Steep Cove neighbor asked if I wanted a day of work. Jay, sixty-something, was strongly built with bristly gray hair and blue eyes. He had purchased a load of locally cut lumber to expand his house, but the wood was green so he needed to give it a couple of years to dry first. He wanted help stacking it in his shed.

We hoisted each pungent spruce board out of his skiff, him on one end and me on the other, and carried it to his shed, talking the whole time.

We got on the subject of a kind of lox he makes, called cold-smoked salmon. Never guessing at the intricacies of such an undertaking, I casually asked him how he makes it.

His face became simultaneously serious and alight. "You need to set aside a couple of weeks," he said. "You can't just run off and leave it."

"A couple of weeks!"

"Yeah, and you want to do this in your colder weather, when it's crackly out." We set the board down and went to get the next one. "And you want to use only prime king salmon."

"Which ones are prime?" I asked. To me, they all were.
~~~~~

"The mature fish, the spawners," he said. "Firm flesh."

We moved a lot of wood while on this subject. He described how he cut the fish in strips and layered them in a tub with salt, and then added water until they were covered in brine. "One hundred percent brine—you know it's right if it'll float a potato." He looked at me and I nodded, happily storing this piece of information in my mental "use in writing someday" file.

"Then you brine it for, oh, about a week, to cure the fish. Then you want to freshen it."

"What's 'freshen it'?" I chirped.

"You run cold water over it to rinse some of the salt out."

"How long does that take?"

"Oh, 130, maybe 150 hours."

Hours? I was expecting him to say minutes.

Two things occurred to me. First, given that his cabin plumbing, like mine, was fed by a creek running down a mountain, it was no problem to run cold water over fish in his sink for that many hours. Second, it was bordering on surreal, the amount of time it took to make this cold-smoked salmon of his.

He went on, "You taste a hunk of tail to check it, and when it's right, salty but not too salty, you hang it on a dowel overnight so it dries a little bit, or at least stops dripping. You gotta keep it in a place that's just the right temperature, maybe forty or forty-five degrees."

I suspected we were getting close to the finish line.

"Then, you want to warm your smokehouse to, say, seventy degrees. And then, you smoke it."

"For how long?"

"Three days." Seeing that I was impressed, he gave a satisfied nod. "People have to be awful damn nice to me before they get some of my cold-smoked salmon."

~~~~~

Later, I was looking out the cabin window, marveling over the time and attention Jay put into making his cold-smoked salmon. Of course, if there was a specialty store right around the corner selling salmon lox he might not be so motivated. But there wasn't a specialty store right around the corner. There wasn't even a hardware store around the corner, which was why Jay had bought freshly milled lumber from a neighbor, and had paid me to help stack it so the wood could air dry it for a few years, before he used it.

This got me thinking about the assortment of anchors, half-decayed skiffs, and other odds and ends dotting the beach in front of the cabin and how once, talking to Tom, I'd dismissively used the word "mess" in reference to all this rusty, lumpy, broken-looking stuff. Pretending to be offended, he'd replied that all this "mess" was wealth, how could I not see that?

I had laughed, but now I could see the truth in his joke. That "mess" out on the beach was a form of wealth, in that it offered potential solutions to problems. If a person needed something on this coast and couldn't find it at the thinly-stocked general store in Bellport, they had to fly it out from Juneau, which meant a lengthy wait, along with steep freight
~~~~~

costs, or they could try to make it. Or borrow it, or scavenge it, or trade for it.

Humans could be pretty ingenious, especially under pressure. Inconvenience was one pressure. Poverty was another. And certain traits were helpful in sparking innovation. Things like curiosity. A willingness to get things wrong. Even pure orneriness, in some cases.

Another thing that helped was having time. To get my water running, I had no plumber to call, or even a phone to call on, but I had an abundance of time. And in Jay's revered cold-smoked salmon, the main ingredient was time.

Thinking about time, I realized it did more than allow me to tackle a plumbing problem when one came up. It allowed me to read and bake bread, to notice a sad man on a bar stool, and to hear my neighbors' stories.

If useful items on the beach could be considered wealth, then certainly so could time. This thought made me grin. Because by that expanded definition of wealth, people like Jay and myself could be considered rich. Filthy rich, even.

THIRTEEN

THAT EVENING Tom called me on the VHF. Not to tell me "backhoe" but to just check in. I asked if he had a good phone signal, and he said yes, so I went to town and called him on the payphone, thereby giving us a bit more privacy.

He asked about my halibut quest and eagerly I launched into a description of my efforts.

"You're happy just talking about it," he said, amused, when I paused to get a breath.

"What?"

"Fishing."

"Well, sure." I laughed. "Aren't you?"

He was quiet.

"But it's what you do."

"I like everything about it," he said, "except the fishing. I like running the boat, dealing with the electronics, anchoring up at night. I really love being out here. It's just the fishing part that I hate."

"You're not serious," I said.

"Maybe 'hate' is too strong a word," he went on. "I dislike fishing. I just do it for the money."

His words floored me. Fishing was hard enough work for someone who wanted to fish. If it failed to yield pleasure, how did a person deal with all the boat troubles, the weather, the defeat? And he'd been doing it for more than a decade.

My heart was breaking for him already when, quietly, he said, "The whole time you were on the boat, I kept worrying that I was letting you down."

"No! I didn't mean to make you feel that way!"

"I know," he said. "But listen, here's what I'm really trying to say: you have the instincts to be a good fisherman. Maybe you should think about getting your own boat. You could fish it next summer."

I laughed at this and said, "Yeah, right."

Dear Mary,

I'm thinking about getting my own boat, and fishing it next summer.

It sounds crazy, I know . . . but the more I surrender myself to this life, the more the universe seems to send positive reinforcement.

For example, earlier today, some bird poop landed right next to me on the beach—a lot of it, maybe half a cup. So that huge splat—from an eagle, surely—missed me. Obviously a good luck sign, wouldn't you agree?

Okay, well, maybe it's a stretch to think that being missed by eagle poop is a sign to buy a boat, but it is worth mentioning that the market is likely to correct itself. People are saying so, and the general feeling is that next season will surely be an improvement over this one.

So maybe just a little boat.

There's a particular kind of skiff, a Boston Whaler, that can be outfitted as a commercial troller. This guy, Joel, has one, so I'm keeping an eye out for him. He appears in Bellport about once a week to supply up. I'm going to ask him about it. I'll keep you posted!

xxoo

Carole

~~~~~

Word spread that I was looking for work, so I got another job limbing a downed tree and cutting it into firewood rounds. With a chainsaw. Wonders never cease. On a remote island, willingness, desperation, and naiveté seemed to trump actual work experience, and I scored high on all three.

Another day, the fish plant had a freezer barge show up with extra room, so the plant managers hired anyone who wasn't prone. I spent the day weighing chunks of frozen fish and filling cardboard boxes. Someone else banded the boxes and hoisted them onto pallets, and someone else came along in a forklift to drive them off to be loaded. It was fun.

Another day I was hired to use an ATV, along with some chains, and a pick ax to convince several extremely stubborn trees to come out of the ground. *Clearing land!* I thought, *I'm clearing land!* That day was really fun, too.

So, things were clicking along. In fact, they were going so smoothly I completely forgot about my fear of
~~~~~

explosions. Then came an experience that could only be described as sobering—except for the heavy drinking I did afterward.

The weather swung around to westerly. This put a severe chop on the inlet and made skiffing uncomfortable. On the plus side, however, the brisk wind brought some lovely clear skies and sunshine.

Hot, sunshiny, afternoons in Southeast Alaska are rare. I plucked my can of Rainier beer from the creek where it had been staying cool and arranged myself on the beach with my back against a firewood log. It was my only beer on hand, and I'd been saving it for just this kind of summer moment. I had one goal that afternoon: enjoy the sun. I popped open the can and took a long sip, ready for some concentrated basking.

Two sips later, I smelled propane and heard hissing. The sound was coming from one of the hundred-pound steel propane bottles stored against the outside wall of the cabin. These were full bottles, replacements for when the current bottle supplying the cabin ran out.

Hastily I grabbed a wrench and looked at the valve on the top of the hissing canister. I'd seen Tom fix things using a little force sometimes, so I banged on the valve a bit, but the hissing continued. I banged harder. Then the bottle next to this one started hissing. And the next one. Okay, now I was scared.

I wanted to break into a full run and hurl myself behind a boulder somewhere very far down the beach. Instead I forced myself inside the cabin, which I expected to go boom any second. Panting with anxiety, I called Tom on the VHF.

Luckily he came back to my call and quickly offered an explanation. The bottles had been overfilled, and the sun was expanding the gas beyond their capacity. "What you're hearing is the pressure-release valve," he said, and told me I had to find a way to shade them. "Be sure to handle them carefully; try not to knock anything against the bottles."

I took the microphone away from my face to stare at it.

"Call me back to let me know when they stop," he said, sounding worried. This is a guy who never sounds worried.

I ran back out of the cabin, saw some plywood, and gingerly propped it against the bottles to shade them. Then I ran down the beach and hid behind a boulder.

Finally, after about ten minutes, the hissing stopped. Tom answered my radio call and said he was glad that the crisis had passed. Since he was in a patch of good fishing, we signed off quickly. Sweaty and still shaking, I went back outside, picked up my beer, took a big swallow, and sprayed it out on the beach in disgust. It was flat and so hot it almost burned my tongue.

I failed to see any cute lesson in this. My *one* and *only* beer was now *undrinkable* because the friggin' propane bottles decided to overheat.

Now, more than ever, I wanted a cold beer. Grumbling with irritation, I loaded myself and Fidget in the skiff and started toward town. Halfway there, the outboard motor sputtered and died. I had run out of fuel. Fortunately a spare fuel jug traveled in the skiff, but unfortunately, I couldn't twist open the lid. *Someone* with *manly man hands* had tightened it *too damn much.*

At my first swear word Fidget moved up to the bow, visibly upset. In the bucking surf, it took me a long, cuss-filled time to get the gas jug open and the pour spout ready. Then, while pouring the fuel, a big wave came and jerked the skiff and a gush of gas hit my boots. More unhappy words burst from me.

Suddenly I heard a splash, and jerked around to see that Fidget had launched herself from the skiff and was swimming for shore.

Shore was a jumble of sharp rocks. She clawed up onto a rock and turned to look at me, worry written all over her face. Mortified, I drove over to retrieve her, and she kept looking away from me, unable to meet my eyes. She seemed embarrassed for us both.

It took some sweet-talking to get her back into the skiff, and then big promises involving raisins, before she wagged her tail for me. Finally I carried on to town, sweaty and thirsty, and now reeking of gasoline.

Fidget came into the bar with me and since dogs were not officially allowed in, she trotted right over to hide under the pool table, which was our usual practice. I slid onto a barstool.

Next to me was a fisherman named Al. Probably Bellport's friendliest person, Al took one look at my face and reached for his wallet. "What are you drinking?" he asked.

"A lot," was my answer.

He laughed and signaled for the bartender.

Fifteen years older than me, Al had coloring so much like mine—ginger-haired and freckly—he looked more like my older brother than my older brother did. He ordered me a beer, waited until I gulped a long swallow, and asked, “So what’s up?”

I told him about the hissing propane bottles, and he listened with a sympathetic grin. He followed my story with one of his own involving a can of beans. He was out fishing and had just tossed the beans in his boat stove to heat them up—not bothering to open the can since he planned to get it out soon. But the fish started to bite like crazy, he forget about the beans and finally the stove door blew off. “Beans everywhere,” he said cheerfully, and took a pull on his beer.

Some people swirled in, and after greetings and jests were exchanged, I resumed talking with Al. “You’re always so upbeat. I guess you like it here?”

“I like the lifestyle,” he shrugged. “I’m not an indoor guy. You could put me in a five-hundred-dollar suit and I’d look like an unmade bed.”

I remembered that he had a reputation for being an avid hunter and asked if he had a favorite place to go, and he said he had bunch of them. “Uncle Bill showed me a lot. And I’m always finding new places to go.” He laughed. “Or not go.”

“Could you take me sometime?” Suddenly I ached to get up to where I could see sky spreading in all directions. “I’m reachable on the VHF.”

“I’ll probably go soon,” he said. “While there’s sunshine.”

My impromptu bar visit ended up going until very late.

In the morning, my body felt stomped by a hangover—better than completely blown to pieces by a propane bottle, but barely. It took me forever to brush my teeth. I was thinking fragmented, woolly thoughts, brushing, stopping, brushing some more, when an unfamiliar voice hailed me over the VHF. "Carole, you on channel one?"

I keyed the mic and croaked, "Yeah, who's this?"

"It's Al. I'm going hunting if you want to come. Although you might not be feeling so good today." He said this last bit laughing.

I was going to decline, but when he made that crack, of course I agreed to go. Another guy, Gary, would be with us as well, Al told me. They'd come get me in a half hour or so.

My pack was huge. I hate to be cold or to get too hot, so that meant bringing a variety of clothing options. I brought lots of grub, since my metabolism burns through food. And plenty of water, with the sunshine and sweating and all. Oh, and I had to bring a notebook, of course.

We skiffed to one of their favorite spots. Gary set off climbing in one direction; Al and I went up the other. Seeing how lightly the guys packed convinced me to leave half my stuff behind in the skiff. It was a good thing because Al's pace was swift, and we were going through steep terrain that was full of obstacles. It took me no time at all to trip and wipe out on a slippery slope.

"That's one," Al said over his shoulder, and I laughed as I caught up. A moment later he slipped and went down on a knee, which, instinct told me, didn't count. When his backside hit the ground a few minutes later, I waited and let him say it. "One," he said cheerfully.

I had stepped into the woods wanting to prove myself, but relaxed as we climbed. Reaching the foot of a nearly vertical rise, we stopped to eye different possible routes. Any path we took would involve precarious clinging.

Al patted his shirt pocket and pulled out half a cigar. Gesturing with it, he asked, "Cigar?"

"I'm trying to quit," I said.

He lit up and squinted at the cliff facing us. "Now, James Bond, he would just . . . zzzwoop—get himself up there with some fancy equipment."

"Yeah," I said, "and he'd have a Russian blonde waiting for him at the top."

"Two of them." Al grinned around his cigar.

On the way up he didn't try to help me, which I appreciated. There wasn't an extra hand to give, anyway. I slid backward once but caught myself. Like everything in this country, getting up took patience and attention.

Once past the cliff, Al apologized for getting us into such a tough situation. I said it was okay, but it would probably affect his tip.

We finally reached high open country. "I gotta eat," I said, plopping down and ripping into my sandwiches. He declined my offer to share, and looked around with his binoculars.

"There's a fawn," he said quietly.

I stopped chewing, suddenly afraid of making too much noise. "Where?" I whispered, reaching for my binoculars. It took me a while to see the deer. It was far away but was looking right at us, and though we watched for a while, it didn't move. "Pretty little thing," he said. We never saw its momma, but Al assured me that she certainly saw us.

We went higher and talked very little as we scanned the nearby cliffs for bucks. We spent a few hours up there, climbing around the peaks. I ate all my food, plus grazed on some alpine blueberries. He smoked his cigar and ate a few handfuls of trail mix.

We didn't come across any bucks, but Al seemed unconcerned. He told me, "Last time up here, I saw a little forky deer. The forks weren't much bigger than his ears. Watched him for a long time, took a little nap, watched him some more. Had a great day."

We headed back down, hoping Gary had been successful. On the way, we each added another wipeout to our scores.

Minutes after we reached the skiff Gary returned, which astounded me. I could never have found my way back to the same spot, let alone timed it like that. He had no buck and like Al, took it in stride. He asked me, "How'd it go?"

I was muddy, disheveled, hungry, thirsty, and ecstatic. "Loved it," I said.

Al clapped me on the shoulder and my shaky legs almost buckled. "She proved her whiskers today," he told Gary. I laughed at the strange compliment, and laughed again because of the big flush of pride it gave me.

We climbed in the skiff and as we went zooming back down the inlet, I begged Al to take me again sometime soon. "We need to break the tie," I said.

"Count on it," he told me.

I thought this day spent hunting with those guys would rank as my summer's peak outdoor adventure, but then came its match—a day spent with the woman of Steep Cove.

It was one of those days where the angle of light and the smell in the air whisper to one's heart that summer was about to end. I was drinking my first cup of coffee and feeling a bit melancholy when Ginger, the neighbor I'd had over for chowder, called on the VHF to issue an invitation.

"I was thinking we should go check out the nagoons at the secret spot." She said this casually, as though it wasn't a profound statement. Nagoonberries have lobes like a raspberry, and like a raspberry are red and juicy, but they have a unique flavor that is highly prized. And they are scarce. All summer I'd been hearing about the secret nagoonberry spot—not where it was of course, just that it existed somewhere out there, growing berries solely for the initiated.

Ginger said that Flo and her daughter Kathleen had a break in between lodge bookings and wanted to go picking as well. She was wondering whether to bring her rifle. "It's a pain to carry. Four of us should make plenty of noise, plus we'll have Mookie . . ." Her golden retriever Mookie was reputed to be a good bear dog, meaning he'd give warning if he scented a bear.

"And we'll have Fidget." I held my breath, praying she wouldn't ask if Fidget was a good bear dog. Adorable, yes, I'd have to say. A good bear dog? Ahh . . . maybe not.

A bad bear dog is one that encounters a bear and runs back toward you, with the bear chasing it. I could see that happening with Fidget. But I couldn't leave her behind, especially with Mookie in the skiff; it would break her heart.

Luckily, Ginger didn't ask. "Okay," she said. "We should be good with two dogs. I'll leave the rifle behind."

Being part border collie, Fidget was a smart dog, so I had a little talk with her as I packed. I explained how, if a bear appears, she should do what Mookie did. I felt better, once we talked it over.

When Ginger, Flo, and Kathleen zoomed up to my beach, they all wore cocked baseball caps and wide grins. I hopped in, and off we went.

We got to our destination and climbed out of the skiff, four women wearing backpacks stuffed with food, dangling berry buckets on strings. And two dogs that instantly began romping in wide circles around us.

Ginger rigged the boat with an anchor, and then we set out through the waist-high beach grass. Kathleen and I were in the lead, and coming to a meadow, we both let out a whoop to scare off any nearby grizzlies. We'd simultaneously spotted the bear trail.

Bear trails are not typical, faint meandering game trails. They go in a determined line, a series of widely spaced paw prints, etched and re-etched into the land over generations. It's an awe-inspiring sight. It's also a bit spooky, since the likelihood of a bear encounter is higher around them.

We crossed a wide expanse of tall, waving sedge, into a patch of shorter beach grass, lupine, and silverweed. There, we fell to our knees and began plunking the small rubies into our buckets.

Mookie gave a bark, and everyone looked up from picking. "He's just playing," Ginger said. "That's not his bear bark."

A few hours passed. I spent them nibbling on berries, and dropping a few in my bucket when I remembered to. Fidget came over and tried to roll around in the grass by me, but I shooed her away, afraid for the berries. "Go get bear-dog lessons from Mookie," I told her. "Go!"

Lunch was a feast of smoked salmon sandwiches, assorted cheeses, fruits, and veggies, topped off with a smattering of muffins, cake, and cookies. After the eating slowed, we all fell backward in the grass to admire the rare blue sky. I think some of us even snored a bit.

After a bit I heard Kathleen and her mom talking softly. They discussed getting more diesel for their generator, and how their most recent batch of canned salmon came out pretty good, and whether the skiff motor would last another year.

After a silence, I told Kathleen that I envied her because she was raised at Steep Cove, and knew so many things that were practical.

She sat up. Popping a piece of chocolate in her mouth, she said, "I loved growing up here, but it doesn't really prepare you for the real world."

"You mean things like handling crowds? Or coping with crime?"

"Well, I was thinking more like . . . Halloween."

"Halloween?" I laughed.

She nodded earnestly. "It wasn't until college that I

realized my Halloween experience was different than everybody else's. My brother and I wore Halloween costumes; that much was the same. But we ran around our own house."

"You did?" I was sitting up now.

"Well, it wasn't like there were other houses just down the street. What street? And of course, we had to worry about bears."

"So how did that work?" I asked. "Running around your own house for Halloween."

"Well, Dad would start by telling us a scary story, and then push us out the door. I'd be quaking in my little bunny outfit. We'd zoom around the house, get back to the door, and yell 'trick or treat!' Dad would pop open the door, yell 'Boo!' at us, and then he'd give us a piece of candy, shut the door in our faces, and away we'd go around the house again."

"Wow," I said, laughing.

"Yeah," Kathleen said. "Growing up here was kind of like growing up on another planet."

"It's true," Ginger agreed. She sat up and cut a wedge of cheese. "You have these spectacular surroundings and interesting days, but you can get really out of step with the rest of the world." She munched on the cheese. "One example that sticks with me happened years ago. We went south to visit the grandparents in California, and everybody down there was talking about *Star Wars*, and we said, 'What's that?' They couldn't believe we didn't know. Living here is great, but it can be trippy."

"Exactly," said Kathleen. "Trippy is the word."

Lying in a patch of nagoonberries, not far from an ancient bear path pressed into the land, I could only agree.

FOURTEEN

MY DECISION TO STICK AROUND Bellport was yielding far richer dividends than expected. I hadn't felt this alive before, at least, not that I could remember. The air tasted sweeter, the food more pleasing, my eyes seemed to focus sharper, laughter came easier, sleep was happy and deep. I was being stretched, surprised, informed, thumped a little bit, rewarded a lot.

When something good comes along it's natural, of course, to want more of it. I wasn't thinking about uprooting from Juneau, but the idea of fishing commercially from a skiff was gaining appeal. I had no clue what it would really entail, but that didn't stop me from imagining how great it would be.

Finally, one day I was in Bellport and saw Joel, the guy who fished out of the Boston Whaler skiff sitting in the cafe.

I told him I had some questions to ask, and his response was to pull out a chair for me. "Have a seat."

I plopped down. "So what brings you to town?" I began, all chitty-chatty.

I noticed that my fork was rocking a little, and realized it was just him, tapping his leg against the table leg.

"I needed to make some repairs." An odd look was on his face when he said this, but I barely noticed. I was in a froth to quiz him on skiff fishing, especially the financial part.

Peggy took our orders and both of us got the special, a Reuben sandwich. After she walked away, I cut right to the chase. "Joel, can a person make good money skiff fishing?"

"Naw, well, you can do all right." He paused, thinking. The table stopped rocking. "I had this one day last year. It was beautiful, all day long. The water was like glass, and I did really well, got eighty-three fish—fat ones. And the price was good, like a buck-thirty a pound. Afterward, I was skiffing back to town, and the sun was going down over my shoulder, and I just started laughing." He smiled at the memory. "It was a thousand-dollar day."

My eyebrows shot up and a quick check of the math confirmed it. "I want to try skiff fishing," I said. "I just need a permit and gear, and—"

"Most days," Joel said, shaking his head, "it's not like that. It can be miserable. You're exposed to weather, and you just get soaking wet. I rigged up a little cookstove so I can take breaks and make myself oatmeal or something to drink. Actually, it sits right above the fuel tank, which isn't too smart I guess, if you think about it."

I started to think about it, but stopped. "So your days are wet," I persisted, "but your nights are warm and dry, right? I heard you're staying in that trapper's cabin at Sod Cove?"

I reached out to steady my coffee, which was wobbling now that his leg was back to its rhythm. He didn't even know he was doing it. *Must be dying to get back out there.*

"No, the trapper's cabin collapsed. I stay in a tent, and that's another thing. The bugs are horrendous. I get up in the morning and run out of the tent toward the skiff. I look like Charlie Brown's friend Pig-Pen, with that dirt cloud swirling around him, except it's bugs. Not a fun way to wake up."

I nodded sympathetically while busily painting a picture in my mind that was different. I could see fishing my own rig, and then climbing on Tom's boat to eat and sleep at night, safe in the anchorage. I could see it all, except where I'd get the skiff.

Dollar signs glowing in my eyes, I asked, "Do you know anywhere I could get a Boston Whaler for a good price?"

"Um . . ." he looked at me. The table's shaking had slowed some, but now it sped back up. Our food came, and we both got busy eating. He had to be burning every calorie he took in, I mused to myself, the way he kept jiggling that leg of his.

I'd just taken a bite of the Reuben and was doing a pretty good walrus imitation, with sauerkraut dangling from my mouth, when he looked at me and said, "Those repairs I'm doing?"

I slurped the sauerkraut in. "Yeah?"

"I . . . ah. . ." He studied his plate. "I hung my gear up,

caught the bottom with it." His eyes came up to meet mine, and his look was dead serious. "To tell you the truth, I've never been so scared—never—not mountaineering, or even ice climbing."

I had to take a drink of water, my throat suddenly got so tight. Joel was in his twenties and was one of the strongest, smartest guys around. "What happened?"

"My gear caught on a pinnacle, and it stopped me, cold. Nothing broke loose, so I was stuck there." He took a breath. "The current was running hard, tipping me so far over, my trolling pole was in the waves. It was choppy water, so the skiff started filling fast. I put my handheld radio in my pocket and got ready to jump."

I leaned in, tense. "Did the skiff go over? Did you go in?"

"No. The gear let go, just in time, and the boat popped back upright." He shook his head. "You know that expression, 'my knees were knocking'? Well, my knees started clapping together, and I thought, oh my gosh, my knees are knocking—that really happens."

I pointed to my rocking fork and said, "They still are!" hoping it would make him laugh.

He gave a laugh but it was a grim one. "So, now I need to fix a few things," he said, "before I go back out."

The reality of what he'd experienced was slowly dawning on me. Fifty degrees. That was the ocean temperature in the summer. Fifty degrees numbed a body quickly, and then killed it. This explained his leg, and the look I finally noticed in his eye.

I had been sure I wanted to fish my own skiff, just

minutes before, but now, I wasn't so sure.

"Joel," I said, "why do people do this crazy work?" My voice cracked. "It isn't safe!"

He shrugged. "I guess fishing gives me some money in my pocket." He paused, and then added, "and a reason to be here."

"A reason to be here," I repeated. *Good grief,* I thought, *could someone please tell me what it is about this place that bewitches us so?*

~~~~~

Dear Mary,

Nix the boat idea.

First, I *hate* danger. Second, it's a big outlay of cash, when I can least afford it. Oh, and also, there's how I feel about engines. They're hideous things. I believe they should be kept out of sight, under a hood. What was I thinking?

My considerable lack of experience, and lack of financial means, plus the shakiness of the industry, did make skiff fishing a flat out crazy idea. What *was* I thinking? I had been going on emotion, not reason, was the answer. And why? Because this island had cast a bit of a spell over me.

It is weird, sis, how this island life is affecting me. You know when you get in a new relationship? You get swept up, and so affected your judgment goes to hell? You drive too fast and get tickets; you eat strange things; you say whatever comes to mind; you forget you have a job, bills, a cat. That's how being here feels to me.
~~~~~

So it might be wise to ask: Is this a good relationship or a bad one?

I don't know the answer to this question. I thought the life here was helping me gain perspective, but what if I'm losing it, instead? Where is this love affair headed? Do I need to be rescued, or is this how it feels to be rescued?

Argh, this is way too much work. Why can't I just have a conventional life and be satisfied with that?

I am such a pain in my own ass, sometimes.

xxoo

Carole

I put the letter in an envelope, sealed it, and felt better. It helped to vent. Mary would know it was just my way of navigating life's waters. Now that I'd had my little emotional outburst, I could look at things through the lens of reason.

There was something compelling about this life, no question about that. But could I make money here? Not just a day of work now and again, as I was doing this summer, but enough to finance the house repairs in Juneau.

This was a reasonable question. I dearly wanted to be able to fish the following summer, as a deckhand. Even if Tom's operation couldn't support a second person, I knew of at least two other skippers who would consider hiring me.

With regard to this summer, people were saying the fish run had grown strong, so if a fisherman hustled, he might make okay wages, in spite of the poor price. Not great, but okay. Especially in the last few weeks, because by then the fish were really fat.

About three weeks remained of the season. I was interested to see how Tom, and everyone else ended up doing. Maybe the season could be partially saved by a strong run. A high volume of fish might, to some extent, offset the poor price. That was what I hoped would happen. Then, with some downward adjustment in my income goals, I might have reason to try deckhanding again next year.

~~~~~

The fish were getting fat, a good number of them were passing through. That was the good news. The bad news was that the weather was turning, and that spelled trouble for those working on the ocean.

The VHF crackled with concerned exchanges between fishermen as they struggled to keep their hooks fishing during the day, and faced white-knuckle decisions regarding where to anchor at night.

Tom called on the radio. He wanted to let me know he was fine, but admitted that the previous night had been a tough one. He'd taken refuge in Peril Cove, and all the skippers in there set their hooks firmly as possible, but the wind was so strong everyone started dragging anchor. They all spent the night on wheel watch, engines in gear, trying avoid crashing on the rocks, or into one another.

A day or two later the weather bureau sent out an urgent storm warning alert over the VHF. I was confused because I thought we were already having storms, but then came a handy definition which cleared the matter right up. "A storm warning," the announcer said, "means
~~~~~

serious threat to life and property. When outdoors be alert for flying debris."

When the inlet started to boil with gusts, which it did soon after the announcement, all I could think was that if it looked this bad twelve miles from the ocean, the ocean had to be really bad. I gave Fidget some raisins and told her we needed to be brave.

In my head, I started going over all the safety equipment you find on fishing boats nowadays. There were lifeboats, emergency locator beacons, and full-body waterproof neoprene survival suits. When I first got on the boat, Tom made sure I knew where these survival suits were stowed, and how to put one on. They had built-in flotation and attached booties, mitts and a hood. He had tied a pair of sunglasses to each suit. "Why the sunglasses?" I'd wondered. "Seagulls," he'd said.

"One-two, Carole, you on channel one?"

I jumped. It was Flo, my neighbor at the lodge.

"Hey, I was just checking to see that my radio's working. It's blowing pretty good out there, eh?" We talked a bit, and then signed off.

"Ahoy, Carole, I heard you on the radio there." John's gruff voice came over the VHF.

He'd been out trolling intermittently all summer, so I asked if he was home. "I came in yesterday," he said.

That made one less person to worry about, at least.

He said, "It's really smoking out front. How's it looking by your place?"

"Pretty blowy."

"Do you have everything you need there?"

"I'm okay."

Then my neighbor Jay, of the cold-smoked salmon fame, came on. "Yeah, good afternoon, John, Carole. Everything's okay here, just checking in. Carole, you need anything, you let me know, now."

These calls from my neighbors wrapped around me like a warm blanket and I felt cheered. But then I saw a sea duck going backwards in the wind, past the cabin window, and all traces of cheer disappeared.

I tried staying busy. I scrubbed the bathtub. I used a battery tester to sort out dead AA batteries from the live ones. I took apart the drinking water container and went at the Katadyne filters with a toothbrush. Next, I tackled the fish gloves. I filled the sink with water and tried on the forty-three rubber fishing gloves lying around the cabin, and threw away the thirty-nine that had holes.

I ached with worry over Tom, and my hunting buddy Al, and Carl of the busted pancreas story, and anybody else out there, even if I didn't know them.

Then my worried mind pictured a hemlock snapping off the cliff behind the cabin, and I started thinking about how awful it would be to get skewered by branches.

The cabin was getting sucked in and out by the wind, so next I thought about how the walls might just pull apart at the seams and collapse on top of me.

And then I realized that no matter how vulnerable I felt in this cabin, at least it couldn't *sink*. Which led me right back to worrying about the fishermen.

~~~~~

In the morning, Tom called on the radio and said that according to the forecast, the ocean was going to be too rough to fish for the next few days. "I'm coming in," he said. "Be there in a few hours."
~~~~~

FIFTEEN

THE NEXT FEW DAYS we lolled around the cabin, reading and talking. One of the things we talked about was work. The subject of work holds a fascination for me. I've done a lot of different kinds, and love the entreé it allows into various worlds. And I've always liked talking to others about their work experiences. That way I get to peek into more worlds.

So I happily told Tom about all the different tasks I'd been doing for our neighbors, and then quizzed him about jobs he'd held in Bellport before getting his boat.

"Let's see," he said, "I worked on the sewer crew. That was a federal project, so it was good wages. I was also the fuel dock guy for a while." He took a drink of his coffee. "I got sick of that job, so I tried to get fired."

"You tried to get fired?"

"Didn't I tell you about that? About the giant slingshot?"

"What giant slingshot?"

He said, "This friend of mine fueled up his boat, and came up the ladder to pay me for the fuel."

The fuel tanks were on a large deck that rested on pilings, high above the water in Bellport's harbor. Boats tied off to the pilings and the fuel dock guy lowered a big black fuel hose down. When done fueling, a person either sent a credit card up in a bucket, or they scaled the skinny metal ladder between the pilings to pay in person.

Tom said, "We were up on the fuel dock talking, and we happened to be standing next to a pile of huge rubber bands. They're the kind that go around five-gallon buckets of oil on a pallet, to keep them together while they're being freighted."

He paused and I nodded as though I'd seen hundreds of them, when in fact, I didn't even know such a thing existed.

"So," he continued, "we started asking what a guy could do with those things, and pretty soon we had rigged a big slingshot for shooting water balloons."

I blinked at him. "Shooting water balloons where?"

"Various places, but mostly the floatplane dock."

"Wait a minute," I said. "That's at least a hundred yards."

"Yeah, we had to tie a bunch of these rubber bands together to get that distance."

"How big was a rubber band?"

"Oh, about four feet long."

"And you tied how many together?"

"A dozen or so. We tied a big funnel in the middle to hold the balloon. You had to pull it way back and hold it tight." He grinned. "There was something very Wile. E. Coyote about it."

I was starting to get the picture. And it made me laugh.

But then I stopped laughing. "You didn't hit anyone with these balloons. You just scared people, right?"

His expression told me this was a foolish question.

"No way! Who'd you hit?"

"Just certain people. It took some figuring, but we made *X*'s on the fuel dock to mark different launching locations. That way we were able to hit specific quadrants of the floatplane dock."

"So who'd you hit?"

"Well, no one could figure out where they were coming from. The fuel dock was inconceivable, it was so far away. So they seemed to come out of nowhere."

"WHO DID YOU HIT?"

Looking pleased, Tom said, "I got the assistant manager of the plant—he was my boss. Like I said, I was tired of the job, and was trying to get fired."

"Well?" I prompted.

He laughed. "When my boss figured out where the water balloons were coming from, instead of firing me, he insisted on being there when I got *his* boss, the manager."

So, hearing Tom's stories, getting my romance fix, and reading—we both spent long hours with our noses in books—how could I be anything but happy? But, as it tends to do, reality came knocking. It showed up, demanding my attention, making me uneasy. It came in the form of a backache, then a weather forecast, and then a phone conversation.

Tom had commandeered his chair by the window, and I kept trying to get comfortable in the beanbag chair.

The beans had flattened out over their twenty-five year lifespan and were hard as split peas. By the morning of day three, I had a screaming backache but kept trying to ignore it.

The truth was, my backache was only partly due to the beanbag chair. Something else was going on—something I found stressful and didn't want to face.

I was energized by Tom's company, hopping up and down to talk and wishing to do stuff together, while he was worn out from fishing and craving time to read and rest. This was a man who'd suffered months of crummy fishing, a man who did not feel enthusiasm for the work. And when the ocean calmed back down, he had to go back out and suffer some more. I was working hard to respect that.

I'd taken myself outside to play with Fidget, and when I got back, Tom looked up from his book. Grinning wide, he told me, "I just heard the extended forecast for the ocean. It's going to be twenty- to thirty-foot seas out there for the next ten days." He raised his coffee cup off the chair's arm in a toast. "I'm calling it a season."

I had trouble taking in what he'd just said. It hadn't occurred to me his season could end two weeks before Fish and Game normally closed it. "Seriously—you're done fishing?"

"Guys with bigger boats, they can't justify quitting yet, but everyone else will pack it in, I'm sure."

I lowered myself into the beanbag chair. "But the fish are so fat, now." It was an inane comment, but it represented how my brain worked. I knew the fish were out there, milling around, averaging eight, ten pounds. The big ones were up to fourteen and sixteen pounds each. Yes, the price had gone obscenely low, but still, those pounds added up. I was confused by how thoroughly delighted he was, since this turn of events represented a significant loss of income. I asked about that and he shrugged.

"This season was bad, but I've had worse ones."

"You have?" I choked.

"Yeah," he said, "once I deckhanded for four months, and made only three hundred dollars."

My mind repeated numbly, *four months, three hundred dollars?*

Tom stretched and yawned. "All I have to do now . . ." he said happily, "is nothing."

It dawned on me, then. The way he liked to recover from the hustle and stress of fishing was to spend about a month being remarkably inactive. I knew this, but had always been over in Juneau while he fished, so I'd forgotten it. So when he said "nothing," he really meant "nothing"—as in reading, eating, sleeping. These three days were just a preview of the coming weeks. My back twanged and I staggered upright.

He said, "We should get to the store and stock up on food and beer. This weather means there'll be no planes getting through for a while."

Even though the ocean was rough, the inlet looked okay for skiffing, so I volunteered to make the supply run into town. I needed to use the laundromat as well.

I went into Bellport, scowling the whole way. It upset

my expectations that the season could be truncated by weather in this way. It made me feel mad, the same way the decreasing price had made me feel mad.

I had hoped to see a reason to be encouraged about my deckhanding prospects next summer. I had hoped that the end of this season would show that things balanced out. A low price could be offset by high volume. Big, fat fish to the rescue. Now that hope was quashed. Plus, the jarring end of the season hurt in another way. I had counted on having the next couple of weeks to get my head around the change in season, and to anticipate Tom's return to shore. But now there wasn't any opportunity to transition out of my solo time, and into my be-with-Tom time.

I wanted to be glad, like Tom, but that wasn't how I felt. And this business about him having worse seasons than this one—my mind kept circling that, but not quite landing on it.

In town, I went straight to the payphone and called Mary.

"Hey girl," she said, her voice warm. "What's going on?"

Living in the south had softened her Michigan accent, and flavored it with a hint of honey. Just hearing her voice made me sigh. "What's going on? Oh, not much," I said, and then I launched right into it. I explained how weather had suddenly ended Tom's season, and all the tension this was causing in me.

"Tom and I are completely out of sync. He's worked all summer while I've played, and I need to be understanding, but Mary, it's in my face, suddenly, how different we are.

I'm a type A person. I need a project. And he's a type Z. He's happiest in a chair with a book." Then I blurted a question that surprised me. "What am I doing with him, anyway?"

We shared a silence, one of those take-a-breath moments. And then gently, she asked, "Could you have a little cabin fever, maybe?"

I sheepishly agreed she was probably right. We laughed, and it felt good to do so. We talked a while longer, and when we hung up I expected to feel better, but I didn't.

Talking to her did relieve some pressure, but at the same time it stirred up certain questions. Tom and I *were* totally out of sync, and it felt awful to discover it. Because in a small cabin you couldn't ignore a thing like that. Once again, the ground was shifting under my feet, and I didn't know how to find my balance.

Then suddenly, I did know. Leaving would do it.

It seemed odd to consider leaving just as Tom got back to shore but the reality was we needed more space between us. In a month or two he could join me in Juneau, like he did every winter. Everything would go smoother there. He'd be more rested and energetic, and I'd only need to cope with ordinary problems, like the neighbor's cat pooping in my flower box, or a slow leak in one of the car tires.

I rang the airline office in Juneau. The lady who answered confirmed that the weather was keeping the planes from getting through, and the outlook was just getting worse. "So, we're sending the mail out on the ferry."

"When's the ferry?"

"Tomorrow."

This time of year, the ferry stopped in Bellport once every thirty days, so on one hand this was lucky timing, because it guaranteed I could get off the island. But on the other hand, the prospect of leaving so suddenly felt awful, like being captivated by a book only to find out someone had torn out the final chapters.

How frustrating, I thought, unaware that my frustration was about to get worse.

I needed clean clothes, whether or not I got on the ferry the following day, so I went to the coin laundry and was happy to see two machines were free. Then I wasn't so happy because both machines had a slick of gritty sand lining their insides.

Disgusted that someone had washed such dirty loads, I went about wiping the grit out with paper towels from the bathroom. I had just finished when a woman came in to use the dryer, and explained about the dirt. The creek that provided Bellport's water got so swollen with rain that even with filtering, it came out of the faucet gritty from the turbulence.

So I was going to put money, and soap, and my clothes into a washer, knowing the water would be *dirty*.

"It's clean dirt, though," the woman said, and laughed.

My laugh back was forced. *I used to be Miss Suzy Sunshine, like her,* I thought, *but now I'm Miss Pissy Pants.*

All I wanted, suddenly, was a Hershey's bar from the store. Abandoning the laundry effort, I hurried down the boardwalk, but found the store door locked and the lights off.

A sign taped to the window said: *New winter hours: Monday, Wednesday, Friday, 10 a.m. to 4 p.m.*

I stomped back toward the skiff, thinking: *my essential needs are not being met. I need not to be in danger. I need clean clothes. I need access to chocolate!* I passed the dark and deserted floatplane office. *I need not to be held hostage by weather, on an island without services, in the PRIME of my life!*

I started the skiff motor and pulled out of the harbor, knowing I would be on that ferry the following day.

On the trip back to the cabin, I had a lightbulb moment. In one of my letters to Mary I'd asked a question, wondering if my relationship with this place was good or bad for me. The answer was: Not good. I could see that now.

Just like a tumultuous love affair, this crazy environment sent my emotions swinging from one extreme to the other. I was happy, exhilarated, and capable one minute, and the next I felt defeated, irritated, and exhausted. It was incredibly draining. How could that be good?

I had also wondered whether I was gaining perspective, or losing it, and that answer also seemed clear. Becoming utterly captivated by someone, or something, really screws with a person's life. Judgement disappears. Did I need that right now? Hardly.

For the laundry machines to wear a slick of grit, and for my chocolate supply to become shaky, and for the weather to turn gnarly—it was all good, actually. These things helped shove me in the direction that, for the sake of my writing ambitions, I needed to go. For me to stop liking this place was a blessing. It made leaving easier, and it also made it easier to give up any hope of returning next season. I needed to be in Juneau, where opportunities were abundant, and life was easy.

Back at the cabin, I told Tom of my decision to leave. "I know your off-season is just starting, but I've had my off-season already. It's time for me to go make some money, and get on with the house project."

This kind of see-ya-later, we-live-in-two-different-places deal was normal for us, so he took it in stride. He hugged me and said he would miss me, and then he offered to go get the groceries from the skiff.

I explained how we'd fallen victim to the store's changover to winter hours. "Our last night together," I groused, "and we don't even have anything good to eat."

"The tide will be right for clamming in a few hours," he said. "If the inlet's calm enough, we can go dig up some steamers."

The prospect of clamming for our supper—the *romance* of it—caused a happy little skip in my heart.

Not another mood swing, I groaned inwardly. *Oh please no.*

Sixteen

When the tide was right we gathered up the tools and skiffed to the clamming spot. After lighting the lanterns, Tom scraped the bigger rocks off an area and dug with a shovel while I picked the steamers out of the upturned mud.

We decided we wanted butter clams too, and set about digging the hole deeper. His hiking boot had a torn seam and kept making a squirting sound exactly like the critters we were after. "My clam call," he joked, making me laugh.

At one point, I took a break from digging and left the glow of the lantern to gaze out over the inlet. I couldn't see the salt water before my eyes, all was black, but I could hear it breathing, and could sense the life teeming in it. It reminded me of the stories that are within people, and how they typically stay hidden, until someone takes the time to ask questions, and then the story surfaces, like a fish at the end of a line.

So then I started telling myself it was a shame to leave *now*, just when all the fishermen were coming back to shore.

The air was about to become thick with stories.

Stop wavering, I told myself. *You know you need to get on that ferry tomorrow.*

A fish can suck in a hook, but isn't actually caught until its own panic, or the fisherman's yank, sends the barb through its lip. Before the hook is "set," there is that moment when a fish can still escape. It's called spitting the hook.

I needed to spit the hook.

Returning to the circle of lantern light, I asked Tom, "You know that one season, when you only made three hundred bucks in four months? What happened?"

His answer, I suspected, would help me spit the hook.

"It's a long story," Tom warned.

I wanted to hear it, I told him.

He leaned back on his heels, and thought for a minute, and then he began. "Well, longlining work, fishing for halibut or black cod, a deckhand can normally make . . . oh . . . fifteen grand in three months. I hate longlining work but this one year, I took a job. I figured I could handle a few months of misery, because it would gain me a lot of free time to hang out at the cabin."

He resumed digging, talking as he worked. "The industry has changed now, but back then you had your stretches of gear work, mixed in with intense, very short periods of fishing. So before we even fished or made any money, we built hundreds of skates of gear."

He anticipated the question I was about to ask. A skate, he explained, was about six hundred feet of line that lies on the ocean bottom. Building a skate involved tying certain-sized hooks into the line at specific intervals, depending on the target species.

"And you made hundreds of skates?"

"Yep. So April came and it was time to bait up all those hooks. It takes days for a crew to bait up that much gear. Then we got out near the grounds and anchored up, in position for when they opened it in the morning."

"How many of you?"

"There were four of us, besides the skipper. It opened, and we set the gear. Even though the skipper was an excellent halibut fisherman, he was new to this type of black cod fishing, and he was having trouble with the current. We kept getting a lot of tangles because the line wasn't feeding out steady. Then, because of a crew member's mistake, we had eighteen hundred feet of line fly off the boat at once—the king of all snarls. Basically, most of our hooks were not fishing. You always take the season's expenses out of that first trip—money for fuel, bait, and groceries—so none of us made a cent.

"But that was just the beginning." He tossed a clam in the basket. "Next, the boat's engine had troubles, and we had to go to Sitka and get it repaired. While the engine was being rebuilt, we got the gear sorted out and baited it all, hoping we'd get back out there before the season ended. But just when the engine was fixed, the black cod fishery here closed; the quota had been caught."

"No!" I said.

"Well, it was still open out west, by Kodiak, but that wasn't where the skipper normally fished. Plus, the seas out there can really kick your butt. But we had everything baited up, and we were all broke, so the skipper decided for Kodiak. The weather report was crap. I kept thinking, a fifty-foot boat is too small, I don't care if it is steel. But you can't quit a guy like that, plus you figure if you keep pulling the lever on the slot machine, sooner or later you're gonna see some money come out. But I was really worried. You might also pull the lever and get killed.

"It was the end of April and the weather was awful. The night before we left, I dreamed I was a five-year-old girl, buried alive. I woke up screaming, my blanket in tatters. I can still remember the terror of that dream." He was silent for a bit.

"So we started for Kodiak. It's several days getting there and we were going into terrible weather. Nobody felt good about it. Then one night this boat, substantially bigger than ours, anchored up in the same place we did. It was coming back from Kodiak, so we rowed over to get the news. They were giving up, was the report. No fish, and the weather was rotten. If this bigger boat was turning back, it made no sense for us to continue. So we quit black cod for the season."

I stood up to stretch while he continued.

"We had to take all those skates out of the boat's freezer, thaw them out, and take the bait off so the gear could be stored until next year. It took days, of course. We all had our heads down."

I went back to digging. "So then it was over?"

"Oh no, halibut was next. There was a two-day opening in May. This skipper had a long track record of fishing halibut and had an excellent reputation. We baited up, feeling confident we'd make money on halibut, at least. Except a really nasty gale came up. We were able to set the gear, but it got too rough to haul it back. The skipper called us into the pilothouse and said no one was allowed on deck; it was too dangerous. We were forced to cut loose from the gear and just leave it. We limped into Yakutat to unload what few fish we had. No, wait, we didn't have any fish."

"Hold on, you said you made three hundred dollars."

"There was one last opening."

I closed my eyes, shaking my head in disbelief. He wasn't kidding when he said this was a long story. When I opened my eyes, I noticed something in the hole where I'd been digging. "What the—" I said, and used two hands to pry a monster clam from the mud. I held it up for him. It must have weighed a pound. "Is this a geoduck?" I was excited. I'd heard about the giant clams.

He shook his head. "I think that's what they call a horse clam."

"Wow, it's ugly!"

"Probably not to another horse clam."

Sometimes I couldn't decide which I loved more, Tom's story-telling prowess or his sense of humor.

I put the horse clam in my basket and asked, "So there was one last opener?"

"Yeah. Some areas were open for twenty-four hours, and some for forty-eight. The skipper's hot spot was open for twenty-four. You see the dilemma. Do you go with what's known, even though you have only half as much time?

A few more hours can make or break a trip. Well, we went to the unfamiliar spot. The weather was gorgeous—sunny, hot—and the fishing was dead. We were sitting on upturned buckets, deciding who got to clean the next halibut. The few we got were dinky. All this was incredibly stressful for the skipper, more than anyone, but he never lost his temper. That's rare, and I admired him for it. We ended up catching about two thousand pounds, and my share of that was some three hundred bucks."

He stood up to stretch. "So yeah, that season bombed. But it could have been worse." Our eyes met, and I could tell he was referring to his disturbing nightmare. "Wait a minute," he said, "it *was* worse—I forgot something!"

"You're joking."

"No, I'm serious. Sometime during that season I started itching. Got covered with bumps. Fleas, I thought, because there were two small dogs on the boat. But it wasn't that. When the boat was getting repaired in Sitka, I saw a doctor and he said he was ninety-five percent sure it wasn't scabies, but he couldn't say what it was, so he treated me for scabies. Being the handshake disease, very contagious, I had to tell everyone on the boat with that I might—but probably didn't—have scabies.

"This skipper happened to be easily freaked out about bugs and things. I knew I had to do the right thing, but I couldn't tell him, so I told his wife, who was part of the crew. She agreed I did right by just telling her and promised to keep an eye out. I was plagued for months, and no one ever got the same thing."

"So, how did you get over your scabies?"

"They weren't scabies!" He glanced up and saw my grin. "I planned to go see a different doctor and get another opinion, but right after fishing I got work with a mineral exploration company. I spent the rest of the summer and all fall working like a dog, climbing mountains, staking claims, gathering samples. Finally, I got to another doctor and he asked, 'Have you been wearing restrictive clothing that can't breathe?' I told him, 'Yeah, like for eight months.'

"He said it was something to do with hair follicles. I needed to wear unrestrictive clothing and try not to sweat. Do that for months, he said, if I could. I told him, no problem, and spent the winter in my bathrobe, reading."

By now, we'd collected plenty of clams. And I'd gained plenty of perspective to help me spit the hook. I couldn't wait to get on the ferry. Early in the summer, when I'd first decided to take a leap of faith and stay at the cabin, it was a good thing to do. But now I was ready to walk away from chaos and drama and financial ruin. I wanted familiar, stable ground.

We got back to the cabin and put the large clams in a bucket of salt water with some cornmeal. For some reason, the cornmeal made them clear their insides of sand. In a few days they would be ready to be made into fritters and chowder.

For dinner, we had the small ones. They steamed open in a matter of minutes and we ate them off the shell, dipped in garlic and butter. And we talked about how, in a month or two, Tom would come over to Juneau and we'd have more time together there.

Seventeen

I STOOD WAITING for the ferry to load, and a stream of neighbors came up to say goodbye and ask how soon I'd be back. My answers were noncommittal, because I sensed that for me to return anytime soon, or even the following summer, would just make trouble for myself. I was unprepared for how much it hurt to leave, but managed to stay composed, even while hugging Betty. We pressed our hearts together, and I vowed to call her. She promised to write.

John took a step toward me. Looking away over the water, he raised his arms straight out, baffling me at first. Then I realized what was happening. He *wanted a hug*.

I stepped forward. He circled his arms stiffly around me and hesitated, like he wasn't sure what happened next. Then I felt his giant hands go *pat-pat-pat* on my shoulder blades. It was the softest of gestures, but it was enough to choke me up.

John released me and there was Fidget, pressing her bright face against my thigh. Unable to say a word, I gave her a pat and then turned to Tom for a fast, tight hug. It was excruciating to leave, like I was sawing off a limb to save myself from a trap, but I did it anyway. I pointed myself down the ramp, and stepped onto the ferry.

On the ferry I followed the other passengers and got in the cafeteria line. I was grief-struck, but at the same time, excited about the special—turkey, mashed spuds, and gravy. That's what living in a remote place will do to a person.

I slid my red plastic tray down the shiny metal rails, right behind Uncle Bill, the man who, early in the summer, told me the story about the mudslide burying the Fields' cabin.

Bill invited me to sit at a table with him and his wife, Alice. I accepted and it took me about thirty seconds to fall in love with the coy, teasing way these two had with one another. They were making a trip into Juneau to replace Bill's dentures. He'd woken up on his fishing boat, tossed his old coffee overboard, and then realized he'd placed his dentures in the cup overnight. We laughed about it, Bill the hardest, while he covered his mouth with one hand.

My intention was to eat fast, and then go off by myself to do something goal-oriented, like envision my future. But instead, like a baby bird hungry for stories, I opened my mouth and chirped, "Uncle Bill, someone told me that you once fell out of your skiff. And you walked to shore—underwater?"

"Yeah!" His face brightened. "I was heading home after a few glasses of home brew with a friend who lived just down from your place at Steep Cove. I pulled the start cord of my skiff, and didn't know the throttle was wide open. The darn skiff took off, right out from under me! So, into the water I went."

It was winter, Bill said, and he had on heavy boots and a sheepskin coat. And like many people who grew up around icy waters, he wasn't a swimmer. He went in, maybe fifty yards from shore and plunged to the bottom.

"I told myself, *don't panic, don't panic*, and I started trying to walk along the bottom. When I was almost out of air, I'd push up to the surface, gulp a few breaths, and then sink and try to take a couple more steps."

One time he rose to the surface and spotted his driverless skiff circling back toward him. "I thought aha, I'll catch it, but then I sank."

The next time he pushed to the surface, he spied his friend outside his house and shouted just before he went under again. Luckily, the friend heard his shout, rushed to get his own skiff, and charged to Bill's rescue.

"He hauled me in his skiff and was so relieved he gave me a big smooch on the cheek," Bill said. "I was so mad, I almost jumped back in!" Everyone sitting near our table was listening by now, and this last comment caused a burst of laughter.

We stayed at that table for hours. I was charmed by this couple's lively company, and simultaneously felt my heart break a little more. Finally I called it quits and went to curl up in the lounge to sleep. Laughter floated out of the cafeteria, making me want to go back for more stories, but I resisted the urge. I fell asleep listening to the engine rumble beneath me, taking me back to Juneau and the future I had mapped out for myself.

As the ferry docked in Juneau, I thought about the growth rings in a tree. The heartwood forms the tree's central core, and around that, the sapwood—growth rings—form, one ring every year. By looking at these growth rings, it's apparent which years are "event" years in the tree's lifespan. Thin rings indicate slower growth, years with cooler temperatures, or drought. Fat rings point to years with conditions that favor more growth.

By the end of September, if someone had taken a cross section of me, I'd have shown an excessively fat ring due to the time I spent living at Steep Cove. It was an event year for me, no doubt about it.

~~~~~

Juneau was a flurry of fun and work. My housing problem solved itself—a travel opportunity arose for one of my renters, so I plugged into that spot. Plenty of work came my way, so I was making good money. I had fun reuniting with friends, and eagerly got back to work on the house project. It all felt wonderful, as I knew it would.

But some mornings, I found myself waking from a dream I couldn't quite recall, and details from the summer would start washing over me. Flo's head-thrown-back laugh. Fidgets soft ears. John's gruff VHF voice saying, "Good evening, out."

These moments started to hit more often and at any hour of the day, tightening my throat and squeezing my
~~~~~

chest. The deep heat of a hemlock fire warming my skin. The breathing of the tides. The way Betty smoothed John's hair. I'd never been homesick before, but suspected that was the name of this humming tension in me.

I stayed busy, determined to get over it. I even took work I normally wouldn't want. Advertising has never been my strong suit—articles and newsletters, I can do those, but selling stuff is hard for me. "I'd love to," I said when asked to help with an ad campaign for a bank. The bank wanted to emphasize that customers had convenient, twenty-four-hour access to their accounts.

I remember thinking, yeah, so? It wasn't like they were offering anything unique. But I got into the spirit of it, and pitched an approach that touted convenient access, and used the tagline, "After all, it's your money." I thought it was pretty good, or at least a place to start, but my boss heartily disliked the idea. And she didn't want to say why.

I pondered her reaction and could only guess that the words were too casual, too direct. To my mind, a message that was casual and direct communicated exactly the thing intended—accessibility. But at the time, no bank was using language like this in its advertising.

Into my head flashed an image of Bellport, as seen from the air. A triad of islands stood sentry outside the harbor. Their names were First Island, Second Island, and Third Island. That's what people called them, and that's how they appeared on the marine chart.

Straight talk, I thought. *God, how I missed it.*

~~~~~

Busy as I was, Tom and I hadn't spoken much, but that night he called and reached me. He started talking right away, telling me something about finding socks in a dryer. He sounded pretty excited.

"What?" I asked irritably. He had moved his boat phone with its fancy booster to the cabin, so his voice was coming in clear. But still, he wasn't making sense to me.

"I hiked up the dump road with Fidget and saw some broken dryers up there. I looked inside one and found a bunch of socks. Nice ones! And they were clean! Somebody forgot to empty them out, I guess."

Only Tom would *score* socks out of a dryer.

The energy and happiness in his voice indicated he'd rested up from fishing and adventure-time had begun. I ached to be there with him and Fidget. When he shut up about the stupid socks, I wailed, "I'm ruined. You ruined me."

"What do you mean?" he said.

"I've changed."

"What?" he asked.

"I miss you guys. I miss being there.

"That's good!"

"No, it's not! I'm miserable!"

"Well, come back."

Of course I wanted to hop on a plane and go back, but it wasn't that simple. Everyone says, follow your heart, but what if your heart's divided? What if one minute it sings, *Don't worry, be happy. Live in the present.* And the next
~~~~~

minute, with equal fervor, it tells you, *Invest, do something with meaning, don't be a flake.* What then?

Tom called the next night and said, "I found you a chair."

"What?"

"Your chair is here at the cabin, next to mine. It's nice, with a deep cushion, and big, flat arms."

I asked where in the world he'd found a chair like his—with flat arms, even.

"I found it in the neighborhood," was all he would say, teasingly, and I deduced he'd either made it or scavenged it. I had no idea he had noticed my discomfort those three days we spent together at the cabin—we never talked about it. Sometimes you just have no idea what a man is thinking. Especially a fisherman. They're secretive, those guys.

Then he said, "You know we always have a big end-of-the-season bash at the bar?"

"Yeah?"

"It's tomorrow."

That sly dog. First the chair, and now he's telling me about a party. He knows I hate to miss a party.

Tom talked on, about a pumpkin sale the school had, and a piling under the cabin he needed to replace. I wasn't listening, though, because suddenly, I knew that my heart *wasn't* divided.

It wasn't my heart but some other big, fat, fearful part of me that kept sending up fireworks and shouting, *Late start! Hurry up! Get those financial ducks lined up so you can write that mystery novel.*

Nestled in my heart, where that Huck Finn girl-child lived, was the simple truth: I wanted the presence of the inlet all around me, and the taste of fish and venison in my mouth. I wanted to be asking questions at John and Betty's table, and picking lingonberries, which were now getting ripe, with Flo. I wanted to sit on the bench outside the post office just saying hi to people, and I wanted to pester Al into taking me hunting again. Most of all, I wanted to be with Fidget and Tom.

Dear Mary,

I keep thinking about this kid I saw in the grocery store a few days ago. He ran down the aisle away from his mom, laughing. But when he got to the edge of some invisible zone, he stopped, his face scrunched up with worry, and he ran back to grab her leg. But a second later, off he went again, his eyes on the distance.

It makes me wonder if some of us are inclined to live our entire lives this way. We push into new territory, get uncomfortable and run back to the familiar. But then, something inside won't let us *stay* comfortable. New territory beckons.

I'm at the Juneau airport, hoping to get back over to Bellport. My flight's on hold because of the weather. We'll go if the pilot decides to go.

I thought if I ran away from Bellport, I could run away from chaos and disruption, and surprises. I thought life could be tidy and go according to plan, all I had to do was turn my back on all the things this place stirs up in me.

But it's no use. We want what we want.

It's possible I'll never bear down and do the work of writing a book. I worry about that, believe me. I fear something in me is deficient. Maybe I'm not strong enough to stay the course, or even have a course. Adventure is easier for me, in some ways, because it's what I've done before. I've never written a book before.

I'm not sure how long I'll stay. I guess until my bank account (or my sanity) becomes a concern, at which point I'll scoot back to Juneau and regroup. Like the kid in the supermarket, running back to safety.

I'll keep you posted.

xxoo

Carole

The pilot came over to say he wanted to try for Bellport, even though weather might turn us back. We climbed in the van, drove to the airport pond where the floatplane waited. We climbed in, belted up and taxied to one end. After a U-turn, we accelerated until we lifted off the water.

It was an uncomfortable flight. The plane was getting batted up, down, and sideways by the wind. At first it was disconcerting, and then nauseating as we entered a stretch of bad visibility, then got into a pure whiteout.

Earlier in the summer I'd seen a floatplane land in Bellport. A passenger staggered off, fell to his knees, threw up, kissed the ground, and swore he'd take the ferry next time. My assumption was that he'd been on a bender in Juneau, but now I realized it may have just been a bad flight.

It's a funny thing, fear. All summer I'd feared so many things that *might* happen. From a bear encounter to a kitchen disaster and everything in between. And I feared what might *not* happen. I worried that I might not make any income, I might not get the house fixed up, I might not write that novel.

Could I learn to recognize which fears were holding me back from life, and which fears were lifesaving?

The plane gave a lurch sideways, so sudden and sharp it jarred my teeth. The pilot, an expert in risk assessment, sat inches from me in that tiny cockpit, and though his body was alert, I could sense there was no fear in him.

Could I get better at risk assessment? Better at balancing what I wanted in the present, with what I wanted long term?

The flight was rough, but we made it to the Outer Coast. The pilot banked and aimed the plane up the inlet, and we followed the thread of water. At last those three dots came into view: First Island, Second Island, and Third Island.

I felt uncertain about how things would play out, long term. But uncertainty wasn't the terrible thing I thought it was back at the beginning of the summer. It meant there was space for good things to happen; it was an invitation for innovation to drop by for a visit. So, I couldn't be sure what was ahead. For now, I had a party to go to, and I'd see what happened from there.

As we circled Bellport, I spied Tom's skiff cutting a *V* in the water below the plane as he raced to meet me. The plane landed, taxied, and bumped against the dock. I jumped out as Tom pulled up and Fidget, bless her little dog heart, launched herself out of the skiff to dance around my legs. If there was a part on her, it wiggled.

"Fidget," I cried, and flung myself on her. I gave Tom equal treatment, and then we went back to the cabin to savor the few hours we had until the party. My chair was there, sitting next to his. A friend had given it to him for me, and it really did have flat arms and a thick cushion.

It was raining hard when we headed back into town. I wondered if the party might be subdued, considering the season's abysmal price and the severe cut it had caused in nearly everyone's income.

We got to the bar, peeled off our dripping rubber gear and tossed it on the pile mounded up just inside the door. The humidity in the bar was so thick that I could've taken a knife, cut a square out of the air, and wrung it out. Aside from humidity the other thing in the air was pure, unabashed jubilation. I should have known a crummy season wouldn't keep this crowd down.

A band, imported from Juneau, got everybody jumping. The fishermen were hardly recognizable with their combed heads and beards, laundered jeans, and button-down shirts. We women had on dangly earrings and wore tight pants and big grins. There was a lot of flirting and flipping shit and general high spirits.

Gusts of wind kept banging at the door like the homicidal neighbor nobody was letting into the party. "More weather," somebody said after a particularly strong gust, and people started telling stories about record winds.

After a few stories, I piped up. "One time in Chicago, it was pretty blowy, and I stopped to get a newspaper from the dispenser on the street corner. Well, I put my quarter in, got my paper, and as the door sprang shut the wind whipped my coat up and I was stuck."

Nobody said anything, they just looked at me. I plunged on. "I had no more change, so I stood there casually trying to hide the problem, hoping someone would buy a paper and set me free. But nobody did, so I ended up having to flag down a stranger and explain, and bum a quarter to get free." I looked around at my friends. They looked back politely. "Beer anyone?" I said brightly, and made for the bar.

I was thinking, *SORRY, it wasn't LIFE THREATENING enough . . .* but by the time I got to the bar, I understood that I'd received a lesson in matching a story to an audience. My urban friends would have liked the scene I'd drawn, but in Bellport, there were no newspaper dispensers, and there was no such thing as a stranger. So the tale translated poorly.

I was at the bar waiting to order when I spied old, gold-toothed Louie, the town's infamous chest grabber, walking toward me. At the last second, he veered toward a woman standing beside me. Staring at her bust, he asked, "Do you have any Dane in ya?"

She shook her head.

"Do you want some?" Giving a dirty laugh, he wavered off. The woman and I shared an eyeroll, and then I noticed Tom was beside me, exuding his characteristic off-season cheer, amped up a few clicks. Like me, the man loves a party.

"Hey," he said, "John and Betty have invited us to take a trip, exploring on the Outer Coast." His face was beaming. "We can take both boats, and John says he'll show us the way into the hidey-hole."

The hidey-hole was a deep cove in which you could feel safe, protected from even the most terrible weather raging out on the ocean. The route to get in this place was so winding and rock-strewn, however, you needed an old-timer to show you the way.

The band started playing again, so Tom had to lean close to be heard. "We can go hunting by day, play scrabble in the evenings," he said. "You interested?"

Was I ever.

~~~~~

Dear Mary,

It occurs to me that becoming an author is more complicated than just getting my finances together and then sitting down to write. I'm beginning to see that it's also tied in with becoming a certain kind of person; a person who can pay attention, and persist; someone who is trying to be honest about fear, and doubt, and love.

So, I now have a revised life plan.

It's inspired by a phrase I learned while working in Tokyo. I interviewed a man about his effort to become a sushi chef. He described how he wasn't allowed to *touch* a knife for his entire first year. He had to learn first through pure observation. There is an expression for this, he said. It translates to "stealing the skill."

I love that expression.

So, my plan is to humbly place myself in the presence of *one hundred masters*, here on this Outer Coast. My aim will be to absorb as much as possible. And hopefully, over time, this will help me become the type of person who can tell a decent story.

How's that for a plan?

xxoo

Carole
~~~~~

Dear Reader,

This story ends here, where in some ways it is just beginning. To the question of what happened next, the nutshell version is this:

For the next ten years I split my time between Bellport and larger places like Juneau and Sitka. I did fix up the Juneau house but then sold it to buy my own cabin at Steep Cove. It's probably not a shock to learn that's what I did, or to hear that I was completely unprepared to do such a thing.

With Fidget and everybody else I had a bunch of Outer Coast adventures, indulging my inner Huck Finn to a lovely extent. I learned to hunt up in those sometimes unforgiving peaks by myself. And I finally caught a halibut.

And that mystery novel? That actually happened, too.

It turns out that I do truly love writing fiction, above all, and that has prompted a move to Seattle so I can study creative writing. I miss Alaska deeply, but setting my novels in that wondrous land keeps it alive for me.

In the next couple of pages I've included a short excerpt of my romantic mystery, *Bad Guys Beware*, plus some reader discussion questions on *Fishing for Courage*.

Both the mystery and the memoir are available through Amazon, and through my website: AlaskaPageturners.com. The plan is to use the website to post some photos and other goodies for the intrepid reader. Please do check out the site, but brace yourself . . . it's a work in progress, much like my life.

I'm glad you were able to join me on this adventure, and hope we get the chance to enjoy more together.

xxoo

Carole

Now Available!

Bad Guys Beware

An Alaska mystery
featuring crime reporter Kit Finnegan

~~~~~

Meet Kit Finnegan, crime reporter on a remote island in Southeast Alaska. Someone has attacked Kit's best friend. Kit is going after them, and they, in turn, are coming after her. She's ferociously determined, fond of danger, and on a losing streak with love.

Meet Doug Quinn. Hired by a renowned energy scientist to do an unusual job, he arrives on the island to learn that his new boss has disappeared. Quinn is a big, calm, capable man, except with it comes to matters of the heart. Then he has trouble seeing straight.

When they realize they're after the same bad guys, Kit and Quinn team up. But instead of helping, their alliance backfires.

The bad guys are on the brink of escape, and innocent lives hang in the balance. Can Kit and Quinn quit fighting long enough to stop them?

"Bad Guys Beware, set in an oddball town on Alaska's coast, delivers the perfect combination of suspense, action, and comedic romance."

- Quickread Press
~~~~~

Bad Guys Beware

(A short excerpt from the middle)

Nearly every fishing town along Alaska's inhospitable coast had its steam bath, and Nipntuck was no exception. Warring factions of fishermen had built the town in the 1950s. This was back when big money could be made in fishing, but only by the toughest, smartest, and slyest. Those of Scandinavian descent had built Nipntuck's steam bath, and there, naked and sweaty, they bonded with one another and plotted ways to outfish their Irish-American competitors. Their competitors, with their Irish roots, were famously heat-intolerant. They built churches and did their bonding and plotting inside those cool, quiet walls.

Clausen's had two large communal sauna rooms, one for men and a separate one for women, but it also had private steam rooms as well. A friend had held a birthday spa party there, so Kit was familiar with the layout. She dashed up to the desk and asked to see the schedule for the private rooms, as though she wanted to sign up for an opening. She spotted, scrawled in the slot next to steam room number two, "Hamm & guest."

"Oh, never mind the private room," she told the clerk, and handed over her fee to use the women's communal room.

For cover she grabbed a rolling cart with sodden towels and rolled it past the women's foyer. *Move fast, with assurance*, was her motto when going places she shouldn't.

She pushed the cart confidently into the men's area and found the private saunas after a quick jog to the left. She pressed her ear to door number two, but heard nothing. She rapped on the door and there was no reply.

A door to a steam room down the hall swung open, and before the emerging men could see her, she slipped inside number two. It was about twelve-foot square, and had three benches, like shelves, lining both the sides and back wall.

The top bench was so close to the ceiling that someone fit only by staying horizontal. The air up there was so fiery that few people braved that level. Given that the room was filled with steam, if she climbed up there and stayed completely still, she could probably escape detection and eavesdrop. *No way*, she thought, and turned to make her escape. But the thought of Rebecca made her stop.

The burning air seared her nose and throat as she climbed up and pressed herself against the back wall. She had just stopped moving when the door opened with a bang. The faces of the two men who came in were obscured by steam but she had no doubt that the short, squat one was Connelly. His breath rasping, he took the left bottom bench by the door, grunting with satisfaction, while the taller man took the right.

Kit held completely still, trying to ignore the fear crawling all over her skin. She was eavesdropping on a gorilla-shaped, violent-tempered man who was wearing no clothes, and the only thing separating them was ten feet of steam. *What was she thinking?*

It didn't help that she was one of those famously heat-intolerant Irish. Her clothes, hair, and skin were on fire. Her eyeballs felt like they were getting blisters. *Say something*, she begged the men silently, *I don't care if you talk about sports, boobs, or the stock market, just say something to take my mind off this heat.*

"I thought her file might tell us something," Connelly said, sounding defensive.

"Your job isn't to think." The other man's voice was low,

and terse.

Kit presumed this was Hamm.

Connelly said sullenly, "So, you can't use the file, and yesterday, you told me to quit following her . . ."

A mixture of fear and curiosity gripped Kit. Yesterday at the Shanty, her instincts had been sounding alarm bells for good reason. Connelly had been watching Rebecca. And today, he'd obtained a copy of her employee file to give to this man. *But why?*

Connelly whined, "You won't let me help. Why not?"

"You're helping with other things."

Kit's heart rate had been climbing, and now her head began to swim. She ground her jaws together to make herself stay alert.

"But what are we going to do about her?"

In a low voice, the other man said, "It's been taken care of."

Despite the searing heat, Kit felt a chill ripple her skin.

"Fuck." Now Connelly sounded deflated. "I wanted to help. Like with Joan—"

"The matter's settled." The voice was commanding, curt. "We're done here. Let's go."

The door opened, and Kit felt a rush of cool air.

Hamm said he took care of Rebecca. He's the one. Oh God! She had to identify him. She began to get down off the bench, but suddenly the entire room tilted. She went from dizzy, to out of control, to feeling nothing at all.

~~~~~

Luckily, it wasn't long before someone found Kit. A man discovered her passed out, scooped her up and, yelling for help, carried her to a nearby bench in the men's shower area. She opened her eyes to find herself surrounded by a circle of near-naked men. Jungle dreams were something she enjoyed quite often, but they featured Tarzan-like men, wearing loincloths. The white towels and flabby bellies that slowly came into focus convinced her she was not dreaming.

Every inch of her clothing was soaked, as was her hair. Her
~~~~~

body, but especially her face, felt like it had been torched. She was nauseous and blazingly thirsty.

There was some discussion about sending her to the hospital, and this scared her so much she almost fainted again. Hospitals and Kit did not get along. In fact, they freaked her out. She decided it was time to take charge, and doing her best to sound firm, announced she just needed some water. The words came out in a weak croak.

Four men jumped to get her some, and she drank thirstily. Then, before anyone thought to ask how she happened to be in that private men's sauna with all her clothes on, she announced, her voice stronger now, that she needed to pee.

They guarded the stall for her, and then a half-dozen towel-clad guys escorted her to the front lobby. There she encountered a manager who was adamant that she go to the hospital, and unfortunately, he wouldn't budge on it. For liability reasons, he insisted, and ordered her to take a seat while he called for the ambulance.

She understood completely, she said, the whole liability thing, sure. And the minute he turned his back, Kit got herself out of there.

Fishing for Courage:

Reader Discussion Questions

Because I can't bear to part so soon, I dreamed up some questions about *Fishing for Courage* you might enjoy discussing with your book club (or your dog, or gecko, or parrot):

1. Is there a memorable moment or favorite scene in the story that sticks with you?

2. How does this book jive with or change your image of Alaska?

3. Did you learn something that you didn't know?

4. Do you think you'd like working on a salmon troller?

5. How did the hunting scene affect you?

6. Was the colloquial language used in the book a plus or minus in your opinion? Were some words or expressions too unfamiliar?

7. Do you think this book would be enjoyed by Alaskans and non-Alaskans, equally?

8. Do you think men and women would equally enjoy it?

9. If you were to find yourself climbing off a floatplane at the dock in Bellport, after you waved good-bye to the pilot, where would you be inclined to go first—the bench outside the post office, the cafe, the bar, the flats, or to stroll around the harbor looking at boats?

10. What do you think about the notion that when we're young, the things we love, and way we play might provide essential clues as to who we are?

11. Did you find the end satisfying?

Your Endorsement Makes a Difference

If you've enjoyed this book I'd be grateful if you could tell your friends about it. If you use e-mail, or social media, feel free to post the information, a link, a review, or even a chunk you like from the book.

If you're willing to take a few extra minutes to help a fledgling author, I'd appreciate a star rating / review (only 25 words necessary) on Amazon. Just click on one of my titles, and scroll down the book description page to the part that says: Customer Reviews.

Thanks a bunch!
Carole Gibb

PS: I have to add something about feeding raisins to dogs. Don't do it! I learned belatedly that some dogs can react to raisins. Fidget never had a problem with them, but I'd feel bad if I didn't say something.

And Finally . . . Some Acknowledgments

I'm indebted to these kind folks for brightening my life: Most of all, Stew. Also, Betty and John, Gail, Katie, Denny, Gaylen, Bernice, Jake, Karen, Victo, Uncle Bill and Alice, Ruth, Patti, Mary Lou, Linda, Rose, Josh, Carter, Terry, and Red-man. And thanks, also, to those who didn't end up in these pages, but who generously shared with me their thoughts and stories.

It's my great fortune to be in a writing and editing cooperative with three fabulous writers: Arlene Springer, Kelley Beebe, and Leslie Barber. What amazing women. The hours we've spent sharing revelations and encouragement have been priceless to me. I simply can't thank you enough.

Several professional photographers were generous with their work, including Katie Corbin, who took that lovely photo on the front of the book; Ralph A. Clevenger, who took the picture of me picking goose tongue; and David Jensen, who captured Fidget's cuteness so well.

Gery Rudolph, graphic designer, your eye for beauty and your high standards have made this book a visual wonder. Thanks, also to Alan Boner for website help and transcendent tango dances.

Many Alaskan authors responded graciously when I begged for advice, including, from Sitka, John Straley, author of *The Big Both Ways*, and also the mystery series starting with *The Woman Who Married a Bear*; Richard Nelson (*The Island Within*); and Carolyn Servid (*Of Landscape and Longing*); also Kim Heacox of Gustavus (*The Only Kayak*); and Lynn Schooler of Juneau (*The Blue Bear*).

Dana Stabenow and Sue Henry, writers of Alaska mysteries featuring strong women characters, thanks for the inspiration your writing has given me.

Many friends offered support and/or gave much appreciated feedback on drafts: Family members Mary Healy, Sue Zitterman, Mary (Olive) Healy, and Kitty Carrico-Carpenter. In Seattle, Richard Webster, Carmen McCafferty, Carrie Wicks, Donna Denno, Daniel and Kyla Luksic, Evelyn Heaton, Teresa Heaton, Greg Kimberly, Susan Balshor, and Elizabeth Brinton. In Anacortes, Anne Reilly, in Wrangell, Ottie and Chris Florschutz, and in Juneau, Sally Donaldson, Jane Pascoe, Karen Smith, Emily Wall, Lori Thompson and Riley Woodford.

Olivia Blumer lent valuable insight early in the process. And Erin Mock, thanks for the help with the map.

Hugs go to Brad Swanson, for helping me keep to my principles, especially the asteroid principle. Also to Toni Carrington and Paul Olson (especially for that tip about the c.o.) Three cheers for the Homer Brewing Company and Ray-Jen Cajun, as well as the Crabgrass Band and the Bob Family Band. Happy times!

Jane Roodenburg thanks for catching those pesky typos, and also, for teaching me the Root Hog and the Brouhaha wrestling moves at the Alaskan Bar and Hotel and for making me laugh harder than anyone I know. (Harder, even, than Colette.)

Which brings me to Colette Costa. You cut off the bottom six inches of my dress off while I was at that wedding/roller skating party. Please don't ever do that again.

And to my parents, Mary Lou Healy and John Robert Healy, words are inadequate, but I'll try anyway. With all my heart, thank you.

About the Author

Carole Gibb (née Healy) has taken the buffet approach to work. A scoop of this, a dab of that, with seconds and even thirds on the favorites. Writing work is definitely a favorite. She's been a staff writer for the *Juneau Empire*, an editor with Alaska's state wildlife bureau, and has contributed essays to the public radio program AK. Her articles have also appeared in the *Chicago Tribune*, *Today's Chicago Woman*, and the *Washington Post*.

She has published two books, *Fishing for Courage*, which is autobiographical, and a mystery called *Bad Guys Beware*. She's currently working on her next book. You can learn more at AlaskaPageturners.com.

Made in the USA
San Bernardino, CA
23 December 2012